Accelerating
Student and
Staff Learning

Accelerating Student and Staff Learning

Purposeful
Curriculum
Collaboration

KAY PSENCIK

FOREWORD BY STEPHANIE HIRSH

CORWIN
A SAGE Company

For information:

Corwin
A SAGE Company
2455 Teller Road
Thousand Oaks, California 91320
(800) 233-9936
Fax: (800) 417-2466
www.corwinpress.com

SAGE Ltd.
1 Oliver's Yard
55 City Road
London EC1Y 1SP
United Kingdom

SAGE India Pvt. Ltd.
B 1/I 1 Mohan Cooperative
   Industrial Area
Mathura Road, New Delhi 110 044
India

SAGE Asia-Pacific Pte. Ltd.
33 Pekin Street #02-01
Far East Square
Singapore 048763

Printed in the United States of America.

Library of Congress Cataloging-in-Publication Data

Psencik, Kay.
Accelerating student and staff learning: Purposeful curriculum collaboration/Kay Psencik.
    p. cm.
Includes bibliographical references and index.
ISBN 978-1-4129-7145-4 (cloth)
ISBN 978-1-4129-7146-1 (pbk.)
    1. Learning. 2. Curriculum planning. 3. Group work in education. I. Title.

LB1060.P828 2009
375'.001—dc22   2008038967

This book is printed on acid-free paper.

10 11 12 13   10 9 8 7 6 5 4 3 2

Acquisitions Editor:	Dan Alpert
Associate Editor:	Megan Bedell
Production Editor:	Amy Schroller
Copy Editor:	Adam Dunham
Typesetter:	C&M Digitals (P) Ltd.
Proofreader:	Jennifer Gritt
Indexer:	Judy Hunt
Cover Designers:	Lisa Riley and Scott Van Atta

Contents

Foreword

In my career I was honored on several occasions to participate on district-level curriculum writing teams. Each experience was professionally rewarding. And while I believed my individual students benefitted from my experience, there were many students whose teachers were not given similar opportunities. The district tried to compensate for this situation by offering curriculum orientation sessions. However, there were limits as to the impact these one-shot sessions could have on my colleagues' teaching.

Research consistently reinforces that the most important factor in a student's learning is the quality of teaching experienced each day. That quality is influenced not only by the qualifications of the teacher, but the content of the lesson, and the strategies applied by the teacher to facilitate student learning. My experience demonstrated for me that when teachers are given the opportunity to study and design powerful lessons based on standards, more students experience success.

Years later what I learned "in practice" was explained to me "in theory." In 1998 Susan Loucks Horsley and several colleagues wrote a comprehensive professional learning strategies guide for math and science teachers. It was my first exposure to the concepts of curriculum implementation, replacement units, and curriculum development and adaptation as professional development. Considering curriculum development as a powerful form of professional learning was based on several shared assumptions as follow:

> Those closest to the level of implementation are best suited to develop curriculum. Through the process teachers increase their content and pedagogical knowledge and reflect on their teaching.
>
> The development of curriculum provides teachers with numerous opportunities to learn from others who have expertise outside of the classroom.
>
> Teachers can increase their understanding of both content and pedagogy by thinking carefully about the broad goals of the curriculum and the specific content, skills, and attitudes that students need to acquire. (p. 80–81)

For too long the potential impact and relationship of school and team-based curriculum development has been ignored. Too many school systems still hold curriculum development as a district-level responsibility and fail to recognize the potential benefits to sharing the responsibility between the school and central office. Our current system of education is organized around standards and assessments at each grade level. And while ensuring all students are held to similarly high standards, schools and teachers need the flexibility to design the curriculum and lessons that will ensure their students successfully meet the standards. Districts that hold the curriculum reins too tight may unwittingly fail to realize many powerful benefits that may accompany sharing the responsibility with leadership teams at the school, grade level and department levels. These benefits may include the following:

- Curriculum that addresses the immediate needs of the learners. Data driven decision making provides teachers with insights as to the standards that are challenging students and the curriculum that will be most helpful in addressing those challenges. Data indicates what students know and where they are struggling. While curriculum may be sequenced for one particular approach, much of it is better revised when the data indicates students are either not ready for what is scheduled next or can move faster than the curriculum recommends.

- Curriculum that addresses the interests and strengths of students. No independent group of curriculum writers knows teachers' students interests and assets better than the assigned classroom teachers. Teachers provided the context and support for ongoing curriculum refinement are better situated to meet student needs. In addition, research demonstrates connections between student engagement and student learning.

- Curriculum adjustable to the identified needs of students. In addition to strengths and interests, students have unique needs. Once again teachers are best positioned to understand their students' needs and need to feel empowered to make the decisions regarding how the curriculum can be adjusted to meet their students' needs.

- Curriculum that is understood and appreciated by the classroom teachers at a deep level. In fact, teacher who divide up lesson assignment responsibilities as opposed to collaborating in the development of lessons have very different experiences in classrooms. There is no substitute for the depth of knowledge that results from the joint development and assessment of classroom curricula. Scripted lessons can have limited impact on teachers and their students.

- Curriculum that considers the context in which it is delivered. Schools, communities, families, can bring different strengths to a learning community. When teachers are encouraged to develop curriculum that takes advantage not only of their students' strengths but their families' backgrounds and strengths, then they can find ways to engage families in the learning process and leverage the benefits that accompany family involvement.

Kay Psencik understands all these benefits. In fact she has understood them for almost 30 years. Having spent most of her career at the central office level she recognized the importance of balancing the roles and responsibilities for curriculum development in the ways that best served the educators and their students. This book represents a compilation of her best strategies.

Educators who choose to embrace the professional learning approach advocated by Psencik will unleash a *powerful, proven,* and *practical* process. Psencik writes like the skillful facilitator she is. She begins each phase with a discussion of her core beliefs, outlines steps to reach an identified goal, and shares strategies for assessing progress. She is detail oriented out of respect for the many challenges and expectations that confront educators and her hope to help others surmount the problems many educators face.

Psencik creates a *powerful* and compelling vision—all students performing at standard—for school leaders committed to school-based professional learning. Curriculum development as professional learning for teacher leaders is an effective strategy to achieving the vision. As teachers work collaboratively to review standards, evaluate curriculum, design lessons, and create assessments, they engage in embedded curriculum development and adaptation. Over the course of a school year, they create a useful student-focused and standards-based curriculum that ensures all students meet objectives. Psencik's approach to curriculum development offers a powerful job-embedded professional learning model.

Psencik's approach is *practical* as well. Through each phase, Psencik reviews the assumptions upon which she bases her recommendations, then moves to a review of the relevant research base, and finally offers questions to focus the learning team on the critical issues. During each phase, educators are encouraged to reflect, write, and adapt. Psencik includes case studies that demonstrate the results she experienced with the process in many different school settings. The results are indisputable, demonstrating the process can work. At the same time, she recognizes that each site has its unique challenges and she closes with reflective questions to further support the team learning process.

Kay Psencik's approach to curriculum development and school-based professional learning has *proven* results to support it. Her approach has demonstrated impact with many constituencies in diverse settings. Her ideas were shaped by her experience working in both a rural school system and a large, urban school system. Psencik advocated for curriculum alignment and development during the school year as opposed to after the school year, and for professional learning that enabled teachers to understand deeply the standards their students were expected to master long before others were thinking about the issues. The book she has written exemplifies her countless success stories from the west coast in Oregon to the east coast in New York.

Kay Psencik has been a valued colleague for almost 30 years. I marvel at how much she has learned and how much she has accomplished since our first meeting. Enjoy the passion and expertise that Kay Psencik brings to life in this book. Use this text to transform your learning communities—you will gain the knowledge and skills to begin the important journey to ensuring every educator experiences effective professional learning every day so every student achieves.

Stephanie Hirsh

Loucks-Horsley, S., Hewson, P., Love, N., and Stiles, K. (1998). *Designing professional development for teachers of science and mathematics*. Thousand Oaks, CA: Corwin Press.

Acknowledgments

I especially want to thank Jack Reeves and Charles Patterson, two dear friends, who served as superintendents in Temple and Killeen, Texas. Both mentored me. They modeled leadership strategies essential to ensuring the success of all students. Through observing their passions for and commitment to student outcomes, to high expectations for all, and to collaboration and learning of staff, I grew as an administrator. They led professional learning communities long before those were common terms, and during their service as superintendents, the achievement of students in these districts reflected their commitment to teaching and learning.

So many people shaped who I am as an educator: Shirley Hord and her deep thoughtful research, writings, and leadership in building professional learning communities. Dennis Sparks, executive director emeritus, Stephanie Hirsh, executive director, Joellen Killion, assistant executive director, and Linda Munger, senior consultant, National Staff Development Council coached and guided me to deep understanding of the principles and standards of professional learning. I thank them so much for their commitment to student and staff learning and their vision that when educators engage in effective professional learning every day, every student achieves.

I also want to thank those school district leaders and school principals that I have been privilege to serve over the past several years. These leaders have a clear vision of their schools as high performing, communities of learners. I am so grateful to them for all the many stories that we have shared. I especially want to thank Kathy Larson, principal of Heritage Elementary and Victor Vegara, principal of Valor Middle School, both from Woodburn, Oregon, who made fundamental leadership decisions to engage teaching teams in collaboration and learning around curriculum, assessment, and instruction. I am also grateful I have had the opportunity to work with Judy Tyson, principal of Iduma Elementary in Killeen, Texas, who led a new school family to a shared vision around a fundamental commitment to high expectations in curriculum, assessment, and instruction.

Many of the stories in this book reflect a districtwide commitment to professional learning. Linda Reeves, Superintendent of North Marion, Aurora, Oregon; Gloria Shamanoff, Northwest Allen School District, Fort Wayne, Indiana; and Ione Bonds, Petal Schools, Petal, Mississippi; have been models for others of how to build districtwide focus on professional learning communities and sustain the effort through the challenges.

Most important, the stories of significance in this book are stories of teachers and their work. The examples shared in the book are actual works and products of teachers from all across the country who honestly engage in learning with other teachers and who share the impact of that work on their own learning and the learning of their students.

Another gift I have been given is my editor, Dan Alpert. I was always more eager to work harder, more inspired, and more encouraged after talking with Dan. I feel truly blessed that he was my editor. What was most inspirational is his commitment to professional development and his passion for inspiring this author to do her best. I have had a wonderful team of editors and I am grateful for the assistance of Megan Bedell, Amy Schroller, and Adam Dunham for all they have done to make sure my words told the story I wanted to tell.

Finally, I have always been most fortunate to have a family that encouraged me. I want to thank Don, my husband of forty years and my two wonderful daughters, Annette Jones and Erin Psencik, and my son-in-law Ron Jones who have known me as a passionate educator for a long time and who accept me as I am. And I live in joy and gratitude for my beautiful granddaughter, Kate, who rejuvenates me to work even harder so that the world in which she lives is hopeful, peaceful, healthy, creative, and compassionate.

Publisher's Acknowledgments

Corwin gratefully acknowledges the contributions of the following individuals:

Yolanda Abel, Instructor of Teacher Preparation
Johns Hopkins University, Baltimore, MD

Judy Brunner, Instructor
Missouri State University, Springfield, MO

Teresa Cunningham, Principal/Literacy Leader
Laurel Elementary School, Laurel Bloomery, TN

Boyd Dressler, Associate Professor of Education in Leadership
Montana State University, Bozeman, MT

Mike Greenwood, District Teacher Leader
Windsor Public Schools, Springfield, MA

Steve Hutton, Elementary Principal/Educational Consultant
Kentucky Department of Education, Villa Hills, KY

Barb Keating, Principal
F. W. Howay Elementary School, New Westminster, BC, Canada

Kandace Klenz, Middle Childhood Literacy
Moses Lake County Schools, Moses Lake, WA

Dori Novak, Director of Leadership Alignment Initiatives
Maryland State Department of Education

Linda Diane Patin, Aldine Resource Center
Aldine Independent School District, Houston, TX

Thomas Payzant, Professor of Education in Leadership
Harvard University, Cambridge, MA

Bess Sullivan Scott, Principal
McPhee Elementary School, Lincoln, NE

Vicki L. Vaughn, Principal and G/T Coordinator
Edgelea Elementary, Lafayette, IN

Paul Young, Executive Director
West After School Center, Lancaster, OH

Rosemarie Young, Principal
Watson Lane Elementary School, Louisville, KY

About the Author

 **Kay Psencik** is an education consultant committed to increasing the performance and quality of life of all of the nation's school children by facilitating the development of focused, visionary, powerful professional learning communities in districts, supporting organizations, and schools.

Dr. Psencik earned a bachelor of arts degree from the University of Mary Hardin-Baylor, a master's degree in educational administration from Southwest Texas State University, and a doctorate from Baylor University. She has been an educator for over 39 years. She served in public schools in Texas as a teacher and administrators until her retirement from Austin ISD in 1999, where she served as deputy superintendent. Since her retirement, she has assisted school districts and other educational organizations across the nation and internationally in efforts to transform their organizations. She assists them by facilitating development of professional development plans, developing professional learning communities, developing teacher leaders, facilitating strategic planning efforts for districts and schools, designing and implementing curriculum and instructional plans, designing authentic, meaningful assessments, evaluating programs and establishing evaluation systems, and developing leadership capacity.

Dr. Psencik serves as a senior consultant for the National Staff Development Council.

She has published several articles: "Site Planning in a Strategic Context" and "Educational Leadership" in *Association for Supervision and Curriculum Development*, April 1991; "Orchestrating Resources for Students at Austin ISD, Insights" in *Texas Association of School Administrators*, 1996; "Building Facilities to Equalize Opportunities for Kids, Insights" in *Texas Association of School Administrators*, 1997; and "Instruction First: A Process for Facility Planning" in *The School Administrator*. 1997. She and Stephanie Hirsh, the executive director of the National Staff Development Council, authored *Transforming Schools through Powerful Planning* (December 2004).

Dr. Psencik is married, has two wonderful daughters and a beautiful granddaughter, and she spends much time with her delightful friends—Baylor, a happy sheltie, and Brinkley, an 85-pound golden retriever!

This book is dedicated to the thoughtful, skilled, and artistic teachers in America's schools who give selflessly of themselves every day to ensure that all children are learning well, and by doing so, they shape the very fabric of our communities, our nation, and the world. Through their historic, humble commitment to teaching and learning and their passion for children, each of us has the opportunity to discover who we are and to find our place of service.

Introduction

Teachers and principals bring critical knowledge and skills to school improvement and their capacity to invent solutions to the problems of teaching and learning is a significant, untapped resource.

—Dennis Sparks, *Designing Powerful Learning for Teachers and Principals*

According to a story told by Richard Pascale (2000) in his book, *Surfing the Edge of Chaos*, scientists were searching for strategies that could improve the health and happiness of children of poor families in Vietnam. Instead of considering strategies used in the United States and just teaching those strategies to mothers in Vietnam, the team applied a strategy called *discovering and disseminating through positive deviance*. They studied the practices and habits of poor families who had healthy children. They discovered their sources of nutrition, their habits, and the routines of these families. They were on a mission to discover obscure practices among healthy families within the community. After making and clarifying their discoveries, they began to work with mothers whose children were not healthy in these communities to assist them in learning and adopting these routines and using new sources of nutrition. The results were transformational for the community.

> Within six months, over two thirds of the children gained weight. Over 24 months, 85% had graduated to acceptable nutritional status and were no longer clinically malnourished....Essential to the approach is first, respect for, and second, alliance with the intelligence and capacity within the village.... Those whose practices were adopted found their voice and were recognized as a community assets and a sense of self-esteem improved. (pp. 177–180)

I am always inspired by this story. I wonder if there are simple, easy to use, obscure, positive, and deviant practices and strategies inside some of America's schools. I wonder if educators identified the critical attributes of these strategies and applied them effectively and systematically the performance and confidence of all would increase dramatically. I wonder if one of those most powerful, positive deviations in healthy schools might be their practice of daily, embedded professional learning for everyone. When I speak of *the practice of*, I am using the phrase to mean scientific, systematic, and skillful proficiency at something, such as *the practice of law* or *the practice of medicine*—the systematic, thoughtful practice of professional learning.

1

According to Dennis Sparks and Stephanie Hirsh (1997) in *A New Vision for Staff Development*, being in the practice of staff development is being results driven. To be results driven, learning teams determine what they need to know based on what they determine their students need to know. These communities of learners are always asking the questions, what do our students need to know and do well? How do we know that they know? How well are they doing? What do we need to learn to ensure greater student success? In addition, Sparks and Hirsh emphasize that effective professional learning is embedded in the daily life of all in the school community. Teachers, as a community, collaborate on the work of teaching and learning. They engage in meaningful conversations that result in new ways of thinking and new actions.

And yet, according to Mike Schmoker (2006) in his book *Results Now*, few teachers, administrators, and, consequently, students are healthy in many of America's schools. Schmoker's comments are disheartening.

> Almost every class [they visited] revealed the instructional consequences of our historic failure to monitor or supervise instruction and arrange for teachers to work in teams so that they can more effectively teach to clear, agreed-upon curriculum standards. For all we hear about how standards stifle creativity, the very opposite is true. Where teachers deviate from common, essential standards, we see deadening, irrelevant activities proliferating. Years of isolation from colleagues, from constructive supervision, account for this alarming gap between what we know and do. (pp. 16–17)

If educators are going to be powerful forces in shaping America's tomorrow, all must challenge themselves to learn aggressively in their school communities. In the midst of all that educators know about professional learning, about professional learning communities, and about high-quality professional development, it is time to act.

One of the major obstacles to closing the knowing-doing gap is teachers' and school leaders' belief that the solutions to ensuring the success of every child are somewhere outside the school. The continuous search for the best textbook, the annual kick off motivational speaker, and the numerous new, annual initiatives all reflect a belief that the answers are easy, quick, and must be brought into the school. The results of such beliefs leave teachers and administrators cynical about professional development, frantic about the next wave of initiatives, and concerned about the impact of these initiatives on themselves. Educators who look inside healthy and successful schools may discover positive deviance. They may uncover the use of healthy strategies in which teachers are collaborating to plan curricula, design assessments, and analyze student data to determine their students' progress and learning and to design their instructional plans. This work is powerful professional learning. Dennis Sparks (2007) offers the following criteria to guide thinking about professional learning as he challenges educators to simplify and focus on three things:

> Learning focused on clear and measurable goals for student outcomes guided by several types of disaggregated data and other forms of evidence; learning that for the most part occurs simultaneously with the execution of the core tasks of teaching and leadership (teachers and leaders learn while

doing rather than learning about things they are expected to do); and learning that predominately occurs within school-based teams. (para. 5)

In healthy schools, teachers, principals, and leadership teams work collaboratively, challenge themselves to value complex curriculum experiences for students, design common curriculum work plans, develop aligned assessments, and monitor student learning. They begin to use these processes to deepen their conversations and their thinking about their work and the work of their students. When faced with challenges or poor performance on the part of their students, they explore options and develop new strategies. This work is never finished; it is daily work. I once visited with a school leadership team about the journey of changing the culture from one-shot, activity-driven inservice and training to daily embedded collaboration around key aspects of the curricula, instruction, and assessment. I shared that I believe the challenging journey of becoming proficient communities of learners is a four- to seven-year journey. Their response: "We do not have that kind of time; we need solutions now!" There are no NOW solutions. There are essential NOW beginnings—today, NOW, embed professional learning in the daily agenda of each teaching team, and achievement will go up for all students. This learning journey never ends; professional learning that impacts student learning is embedded, daily professional inquiry, study, problem solving, planning, implementing, monitoring progress, and reflecting on practice. Though there are certainly critical attributes of a community of learners, there is no model. Each community fashions itself as it learns together. As communities begin the journey, student performance begins to improve and staff learning begins to increase immediately, but, as with any new behavior, communities have to engage in the practice of systematic, dynamic professional learning. Such a practice is a significant cultural change that requires long-term vision, support, and nurturing.

Most significant is the role of leadership throughout the organization. If efforts to build professional learning communities are to be sustained, those who lead must always be encouraging, inspiring, and supportive when challenges arise. They must facilitate controversy and remove barriers. They must constantly be building leadership throughout the organization. Most important, they must keep the values and vision clear to all. Leaders who not only value learning but also engage in a learning journey of their own are models of what they want to see in others. Leaders who value professional learning and hold the vision of results-driven, job-embedded professional learning maximize use of resources to achieve the goal. They build alliances with teachers' organizations, school boards, fellow principals, and teacher leaders to keep the focus on student and staff learning vibrant and central to the district's and school's work.

This book is written to assist teachers and principals in designing professional development within their schools that is focused on collaborative systems to design common, complex curricula for all students. As teachers and administrators engage in learning together through their curriculum focus, they better understand their learners, what students are to learn, and what quality work looks like. They share ideas on effective instructional strategies, on assessing students, on monitoring student learning, and on analyzing their students' work. They naturally use this information to reflect on their practice, make modifications in their work, and explore new ways of teaching. My aspiration is that this book will assist school teachers and principals in using simple systems that are within their circle of influence to guide school teams to engage in the work and learn by doing.

HOW TO USE THIS BOOK

I have designed *Accelerating Student and Staff Learning: Purposeful Curriculum Collaboration* as a tool for school teaching teams, teacher leaders, and principals to use to design meaningful professional learning that leads to the development of school-based curricula. In Chapter 1, I discuss my basic assumption that curriculum design is professional learning. The first part of the chapter is to clarify the vision. The other aspect of the chapter is to lead the reader to see that through purposeful and reflective conversations about what students are to know and do, teachers begin to learn from each other thoughtful strategies for meeting the needs of their learners.

Each of the following chapters is designed for teacher teams, teacher leaders, and principals to guide learning communities through

- the process of removing barriers by clarifying and confronting their assumptions about learning and learners and about professional development (Chapter 2);
- processes for clarifying and targeting state and national content standards, establishing complex standards, and determining undergirding concepts (Chapter 3);
- designing annual work plans or curriculum maps (Chapter 4);
- designing assessment strategies (Chapter 5);
- designing instruction (Chapter 6);
- analyzing student work and monitoring student learning (Chapter 7);
- developing grading systems and using effective parent reporting processes (Chapter 8); and
- focusing on the role of leadership in transforming schools and sustaining the work of using curricula as tools for learning (Chapter 9).

WHAT THIS BOOK IS NOT!

This book is not a quick fix or a program; it is a series of learning systems that, if implemented effectively, become part of daily life in the school—a natural part of everyone's work to ensure the success of all students and the continued learning of all staff.

ORGANIZATION OF THIS BOOK

Each chapter begins with a thought-provoking quote, assumptions that support the concepts of the chapter, a brief review of the research, and focused questions to stimulate thinking. I share challenge strategies to guide teams through step-by-step processes with charts and examples as well as stories sufficient for teams to understand and use the processes successfully. At the end of each chapter, reflective questions review the major concepts. Also included are strategies for teams to use to extend their learning. Several forms and tools that teams may find useful to assist them in their learning appear at the end of the book in the resources.

1

An Overview

Collaborative Curriculum Design as Professional Learning

Traditional models and traditional perceptions get in the way of our seeing things differently.

—Thomasina D. Piercy, *Compelling Conversations*

We live our lives and do our jobs based on a huge internal data base of assumptions and ideas, but we usually aren't very aware of what they are or how they shape our behavior. As artisans and practitioners, we have not taken the time and discipline to examine the underlying principles that guide our success.

—Noel Tichy, *The Cycle of Leadership*

Throughout the many shifts in purposes of education and legislation, national, state, and local, as well as the deeply embedded historical discourse, educators are challenged to sift through all of the assumptions and ideas that impact teaching and learning and to call into question those assumptions that are barriers to student and staff learning. Throughout this chapter and those that follow, my wish is that teaching teams spend significant time surfacing unquestioned principles and assumptions that are deeply rooted in the culture of the school and reevaluate those that are impeding the progress of the community.

ASSUMPTIONS

Assumptions, undergirding principles, or beliefs held by individuals and communities are either generative or barriers. These deeply held beliefs often prevent us from seeing with new eyes and being different observers of the world. If educators view curriculum design processes as professional learning, they hold the following assumptions:

- As all teachers and administrators in a school engage in meaningful conversations about their work and the work of their students, they journey into purposeful, powerful professional learning.
- Professional learning communities that are successful with all students engage everyone in the school in working on developing common curriculum, common assessment strategies, and high-yield instructional practices to ensure that they are clear about what students are to learn and how well students are learning.
- They believe that the quality of their work and their learning together directly impacts student learning. They never give up on any student. Students know it because the staff members are continuously, skillfully adopting new instructional strategies to extended opportunities for them to learn. They are purposefully engaging their students in conversations about the quality of their work.
- These professional learning teams are in continuous inquiry and are persistent about reflecting on their practice. They are purposefully engaged in continuous study together to make precise, thoughtful modifications in their work.

THE CHALLENGE OF DEVELOPING A SHARED VISION OF CURRICULUM DESIGN AS PROFESSIONAL LEARNING

Many educators have a very distinct assumption that professional development is attending a workshop, going to a conference, or taking training from an outside expert. Because this vision of professional development is so deeply ingrained, educators are challenged to see differently. School communities are challenged to understand that daily collaborative work to educate all children is professional learning. If teams would seek those organizations that exhibit positive deviance in their community, they would discover healthy organizations whose members work closely together and who sense not only their control but also their power in educating all students well.

Professional learning communities have been the subject of much research over the past few decades (DuFour & Eaker, 1998; Hall & Hord, 2001; Hord & Sommers, 2008). Pervasive throughout the literature is the concept that professional learning communities that develop a sense of internal control over their own learning achieve greater success with all students. These communities engage in collective inquiry and continuous collaboration. They have an intense focus on student outcomes, are data driven, share common visions and values, and are intensely focused on those systems that they control: curriculum, assessment, instruction, and extended learning opportunities for students. These communities value and are skilled in collaboration and celebrations. They are self-sustaining, energized, and generative organizations.

The principals, the school leadership team, and teacher leaders in these communities skillfully nurture and sustain the community by leading all in the school to stay focused on student outcomes and the role they play in impacting student learning. They work diligently to ensure that the norms and values of the community are lived by all, foster collaboration, and embed professional learning. They guide the community to share stories of successes and celebrate their efforts. They understand change theory, manage time and resources to support the community, build alliances, are persistent, and remove barriers. They model what they want to see in others (Blankstein, 2004; Glatthorn, 2000; Hirsh & Killion, 2007; Marzano, Waters, & McNulty, 2005).

The challenge for those wishing to shift their school to one of collaboration and student success is to find schools that are honestly on a pathway to becoming powerful professional learning communities—the positive deviance. Educational researchers and leaders, such as Gene Hall, Shirley Hord (2001), Shirley Hord and Bill Sommers (2008), Dennis Sparks (2006), and Mike Schmoker (2006), all reference the discrepancy between what educators know to do and what they are actually doing. And yet, educators are still challenged to close the knowing/doing gap—knowing what high-quality professional development really is and actually ensuring that every day, every staff member in the school is meaningfully engaged in it. Though educators know that teaching teams who work collaboratively on the essential curriculum increase student achievement and staff learning, many schools leave curriculum work to district-level leaders or focus on using textbooks as their curriculum. Though educators know that teaching teams who use common assessments make better decisions about instruction, many school leaders allow teachers to work in isolation and develop individual assessment strategies. Though educators know that teaching teams who analyze student work and monitor student progress regularly are more successful with all children, many schools provide little or no time for such daily community study and work, collaboration, and reflection on their practices.

Those communities that are most successful at professional learning do not focus their attention on taking training, going to workshops and conferences, or adding a few new strategies to their instructional tool kit. These communities regularly see themselves as continuous learners who learn through the thoughtful work of shaping and redesigning all of the systems that impact student learning: curriculum, assessment, instruction, and extended learning opportunities for students.

FOCUS QUESTIONS

- How do school leadership teams capture a vision of all teaching teams in the school engaged daily in curriculum design, as they are engaged in professional learning?
- How do school leadership teams facilitate the community of learners to focus on the essential work that increases student learning?

A VISION

Powerful professional learning communities have clarity about who they are and their roles and responsibilities for increasing student learning. They view themselves as eager and aggressive learners who

- share the responsibilities of leadership;
- hold high expectations for all staff to engage in the community and gently confront lack of commitment to the vision;
- intensely focus on student outcomes and use multiple sources of data to drive community decisions;
- develop shared values and vision about the work of the professional learning community;
- assess regularly their strengths and weaknesses, their assets and challenges, in successfully moving toward their vision;
- systematically, purposefully
  - o study state and national content standards and establish targeted, complex standards for their grade level or course of study;
  - o establish grade-level or course curriculum maps or annual work plans that determine the pacing of those targeted standards;
  - o determine the undergirding principles or concepts that make those standards essential learnings for all students;
  - o select content and instructional materials that are intriguing to students and assist them in learning those standards and concepts;
  - o design common formal and informal assessment strategies;
  - o develop task analyses and rubrics or scoring guides to assess student work;
  - o select anchor works or exemplars for students to use to assess the quality of their own work;
  - o regularly monitor the progress of their students in learning the standards and concepts; and
  - o design instruction and extended learning opportunities to ensure students are learning what is essential to learn; and
- they take full responsibility for the quality of their work and the work of their students. They reflect on their own work continuously to modify their practice and determine areas for team learning.

Figure 1.1 Comparing Traditional Approaches to Professional Development With the Professional Learning Community

Traditional Perspectives	Professional Learning Communities
• Staff members are in isolation or in small teams that focus predominately on student behavior. • The staff views itself as only loosely responsible for student outcomes and often believes that the reason students are not successful is result of a lack of student effort. • Teachers often work in isolation to plan their instruction and rarely participate in study, discovery, or planning with others.	• Staff members are continuously engaged in systematic, meaningful conversations and share ideas and strategies with each other to enhance the quality of teaching of everyone in every classroom. • The community anchors itself in a culture of high expectations and high performance for themselves and for their students. They hold constant a norm that learning together strengthens everyone in the community. • Each team member makes significant contributions to the success of all. They honor individual student and team needs, interests and goals, and engage purposefully

Traditional Perspectives	Professional Learning Communities
• The teachers look to the textbooks, district-developed curriculum documents, or state documents to guide their work.	in problem solving, experimentation, observation, study, and planning to nurture and sustain conceptual learning.
• There is no coherence or alignment of the curriculum or instructional practices from classroom to classroom, course to course. Even though many individual teachers value real-life connections and global perspectives for their students, they often stand out among their peers as either master teachers or zealots.	• The community focuses on the essential work: curriculum, assessment, instruction, and student outcomes. • The team designs challenging, complex curricula together that engages students in exploring a global perspective, makes real-life connections, and creates responsible citizens. They use multiple resources to assist them in this study and design: state curriculum, national content standards, needs of their community, state, and nation. They capitalize on the expertise and deep understanding of the concepts and principles of their content areas, and the thinking and expertise of others in the field.
• Teachers assign work, grade the work, and prepare for the next unit. There is very little thought about what concepts or competencies students are failing to understand and little thought of designing extended strategies for ensuring students become proficient in what they are missing. Though the individual teachers often reflect on their units and lessons and make modifications in them, they rarely discuss their ideas with anyone else.	• The team systematically monitors student learning and explores ways to ensure the success of every person. They are continuously reflecting on their work, making modifications, and exploring areas of study to assist them in increasing the effectiveness of their practice. • Knowing the power of social and emotional well-being in any community, the professional learning community nurtures the physical, mental, emotional, nutritional, and social facets of life that undergird and nurture success for all. They develop personal relationships with students to know them well and to support and strengthen their total well-being.
• The stress level of all staff may be high. The common conversation is about low morale. Fear exists among staff members about their future in the organization, and people are reluctant to share formally anything with anyone in the school or ask for help when they feel unsuccessful.	• The learning community assumes a vital responsibility for building and inspiring skillful leadership throughout the organization, among students, staff, parents, and community. The principals play a key role in being the model learners. They value learning and the contributions of all in the school. They build alliances with students, the school leadership team, the leadership of teacher organizations, key informal leaders in the school, and parents and community to sustain the vision and to understand the progress of the learning community.
• Staff members view the principal as the leader and look to this person for answers and directions.	• The central office support staff members, including the superintendent, are focused on nurturing principals to lead professional learning communities. They, too, establish systems for learning in which they engage collaboratively with principals, facilitate principals working with each other, engage in study together, and apply strategies that develop and sustain change.

CHALLENGE STRATEGIES

Throughout the rest of this book, each chapter will include challenge strategies to guide professional learning communities on their "learning by doing" journey. The strategies themselves are designed to be simple and easy to use. The challenge for any community is to commit to deep reflective thought, to work diligently together, and to change the practices of the team in their school and in all classrooms—to engage in the practice of authentic, powerful professional learning.

The Challenge Strategy for the Book

1. Explore, as a community, each of the assumptions at the beginning of each chapter. Question them. Debate them. Come to your own assumptions and write them down clearly. If desired, use Resource A, Generating Assumptions, and see an example of the assumptions or principles of the National Staff Development Council in Resource B to guide others through the process. Ask staff members to write their assumptions before coming to an initial session to discover commonalities and to debate differences. Seek common ground on generative assumptions to guide the work of the community.

2. Discuss the community's assumptions regularly and make changes or additions to them as the community continues its work on its learning journey. By doing so, the community begins its journey in building a shared vision of itself as a learning team.

3. Establish a system for the professional community members to reflect individually on their new practices, their work, and their learnings throughout the journey. Consider providing a journal for each member, a diary board, a blog, a common community journal, or a reflecting box for individual responses kept in the teaching workroom area or in the professional library area. Share these reflections on a regular basis during staff meetings or during common planning and collaboration time.

4. As a community, consider the essential questions at the beginning of each chapter. Add your own questions. Delay the answering of them until after the team has conducted research and study, worked through the suggested challenge strategies, and reflected on what they are learning and doing. Respond to the questions as a community and record reflections and comments. Keep a running chart. Select any of the following reflective questions, or design your own. *What did we know? What do we know now? and, What we are exploring and hoping to learn? What implications does this have for our practice? How will our practice change? What visible evidence would an outsider identify as the changes we have made in our practices?*

5. Review the suggested challenge strategies. Analyze the team's strengths and weaknesses based on the assumptions and essential questions. Determine the most effective strategies that best meet the needs of the team. Modify the challenge strategies suggested, or design your own.

6. Monitor the progress of the teams regularly to celebrate successes, make modifications in the strategies, and reflect on what the community is learning. Record the reflections and begin to gather data about changes in the team: new assumptions that we are adopting, new strategies we are using, and new attitudes that we have developed. Authentically celebrate these shifts. Celebrations build energy for learning and risk taking.

7. Review the assumptions and make revisions before proceeding to the next chapter. Begin to declare the vision that is emerging of the team as a professional learning community. See an example of a school's vision of itself as a professional learning community in the Resource C.

8. Celebrate the work and successes of the team; challenge everyone to engage energetically in the next chapter.

Until these eight challenge strategies become a new practice or habit, review them prior to beginning each new chapter.

A STORY

Heritage Elementary is a large elementary school with a very diverse student and staff population in Woodburn, Oregon, just outside of Portland in the heart of the Willamette Valley. Their student population is approximately 42% Hispanic, 33% Russian immigrant, 25% Anglo and Other. Annually, approximately 90% of the students qualify for free and reduced lunch. Far more students' first language is Russian or Spanish than English. After several years of poor performance on state assessments, the school leadership team began to shape a vision for their school. They worked with their district's mission and core values to establish high expectations for their students and to embrace the diversity in the school. They committed to establishing a professional learning community to take responsibility for the success of every child and to learn what they needed to learn to increase student performance on standardized tests. The leadership team applied for a state grant to achieve their goals. Their school leadership team challenged itself to facilitate the learning of everyone in the school and to monitor the progress of each grade level. They established a clear vision of the transformation. The school would develop and continuously work on

- common curriculum that was meaningful and challenging to the students;
- common assessments that expected students to show what they were learning in real world applications;
- informal assessments to check progress on skills acquisition tested on the state test;
- instruction that was literacy based, regardless of the content, and mindful of the second language learner; and
- engaging the students' parents as partners in their children's learning.

In addition, the leadership team established a curriculum articulation/alignment K–5 team that would ensure high standards and expectations for every child, curriculum articulation from grade level to grade level, and elimination of curriculum gaps and overlaps between units of study and between grade levels.

They began their work with an extensive analysis of their state's curriculum and assessment targets. Each grade-level team established common curriculum maps, common assessments, and common units of study. They hired an outside consultant to facilitate them through the process. She worked with each grade-level team for several years, several times a year. The curriculum articulation committee, representing each grade level, shared each grade level's map and discussed whether or not expectations for each grade level were high enough, whether there was enough emphasis on writing across the curriculum, whether or not the mathematics and science curriculum standards were sufficiently integrated with language arts, and any curriculum issue that would ensure high expectations for all students. They also analyzed whether or not assessment strategies were aligned with the standards. They explored whether or not curriculum expectations and assessment strategies were meaningful to students. They gave students multiple opportunities to show what they knew as well as what they did not know. The team made recommendations regularly for changes in the work of each grade level.

As the grade-level teams worked several years on their annual work plans or curriculum maps, they developed essential questions to guide the inquiry of students each trimester. These teams designed and used common culminating demonstrations for each unit of study that led students to answer the essential questions. In addition, they designed informal, statelike assessment instruments, became effective users of the state's test specifications and online assessments, and used their teacher-designed assessments to monitor the progress of their students on state test targeted standards.

As they studied together, they became more concerned about their instruction. In their learning communities, they determined a need for and engaged in long-term, extensive training from national leaders in literacy development and second-language acquisition. These training programs offered extensive follow-up. The leadership team continued to access these resources for several years until the entire staff had competence using the strategies in their classrooms. They conducted walk-throughs regularly to check their progress in implementing these new strategies in all classrooms. In addition, they established literacy and second-language-learner coaches to assist teachers in using these strategies effectively and to continue their own study. These coaches began their own learning journey. Currently, they meet regularly to support each other, to study together, to practice coaching others, to seek training when needed, and to develop coaching strategies for assisting teachers in using the agreed-upon strategies. They became a community of learners.

As they felt more confident about their curriculum, and with the support of their coaches, grade-level teams began to plan instruction together. The teams were often challenged by their own work. The old assumption that doing things together killed individual teacher creativity kept interfering. The assumption was often discussed in team meetings:

> We do not have to do the same things together. It doesn't matter how we each teach; just that our students achieve the same outcomes. But Routman does say that there are certain strategies that develop better literacy skills in students. So does Harwayne and Miller.

Teams had to constantly remind themselves that the research they were doing clearly stated, "We are better, more creative, when we work together. We are most systematic in implementing the strategies that we are learning when we design lessons together. We learn exponentially when we share with each other."

They started their instructional design with their curriculum maps and common assessment strategies. They designed instructional plans that they would all follow week by week, day by day. They debated with each other about the most effective instructional strategies for each unit to achieve the expected outcomes for students. To determine the most powerful strategies for their students, they studied authors' works together, such as *Conversations* by Regie Routman (2000), *Going Public* by Shelley Harwayne (1999), *Subject Matters* by Harvey Daniels and Steven Zemelman (2004), *Mosaic of Thought* by Keene and Zimmerman (1997), *Reading with Meaning* by Debbie Miller (2002), *Significant Studies for Second Grade* by Karen Ruzzo and Mary Anne Sacco (2004), and many more. As they studied, they applied what they were learning through their readings, and they revised their instructional plans. They intentionally tried new strategies together that they were learning from their readings and reflected on the impact of that work on student learning. I will always remember overhearing kindergarten teachers who had been reading about strategies to increase silent reading time for first graders. They decided they wanted their kindergarten students to begin using the same skills. As they planned their lessons together, implemented them, and reflected on their work, they shared what they were learning:

> We need to slow down. Kindergarten students can spend time reading silently, but we need to give them more time at the start to explore the books together. We just need to persist. Each time we have students use this strategy, they get better! We just need to be patient and give them more opportunities to practice. They are really becoming readers. Let's redesign next week to allow for more exploration of books by the students first.

The principal played a significant role in all their team meetings. She often was a participant. Her questions would generate new ideas, move a strategy along, or lead the team to think more deeply about their work. Once, when I was in her office, she could not wait to tell me about her plan. The team was learning a new instructional strategy, and she was to try out the strategy first in the classroom. She had found several great poetry selections that she was going to use, and she and the teaching team had designed a lesson together that she thought really applied the strategy well. She would take the risk first.

Since all in the community truly believed parents were essential partners with them in the success of their children, all grade-level teams began hosting regular parent nights for students to share what they were learning. Students shared their writings, their scientific inquiries, their learnings about Oregon history, and their love of art. And, of course, all these parent nights were in three languages. At one such parent night, I had the opportunity to sit with a young first-grade student who enthusiastically was explaining to me what she was learning about the habitats of ocean mammals. The book that she had written was in a mixture of Spanish and English. I was struggling with the Spanish, so she took on the responsibility of teaching me the Spanish vocabulary so that I would understand. A first grader!

As all of the teams in the school became more and more systematic and purposeful in their work, they began to assess how well they were doing in achieving their vision. They began to post their students' work, pictures of parent nights and student productions, and their progress on achieving their goals in the hallways and around the media center in the middle of the school. All who were in the school or visited it could see the students' work and progress.

The journey was not, nor is it now, an easy one. The teams often struggled with many issues. Sometimes they worked on getting along with each other. When they felt that they were not accomplishing what they set out to achieve fast enough, they sometimes lost energy. Sometimes they pushed back when they felt too much administrative pressure to work harder and move faster. Of course, there were and still are the constant changes in expectations and assessment strategies by their state.

Not only did they experience imposed changes from outside of the school but also from within. Frequently, there were changes in team members from grade level to grade level, in growing numbers of students, and in new strategies and programs adopted by their school district. The school leadership team persisted!

What was the outcome of all this work? They were recognized nationally for their efforts in raising the achievement of second-language learners. They moved off their state's low-performing list after two years of extensive work, and they continue to meet the state's expectations.

Figure 1.2 Heritage Elementary Demographic and Student Performance Data, Woodburn, Oregon, 2004–2007

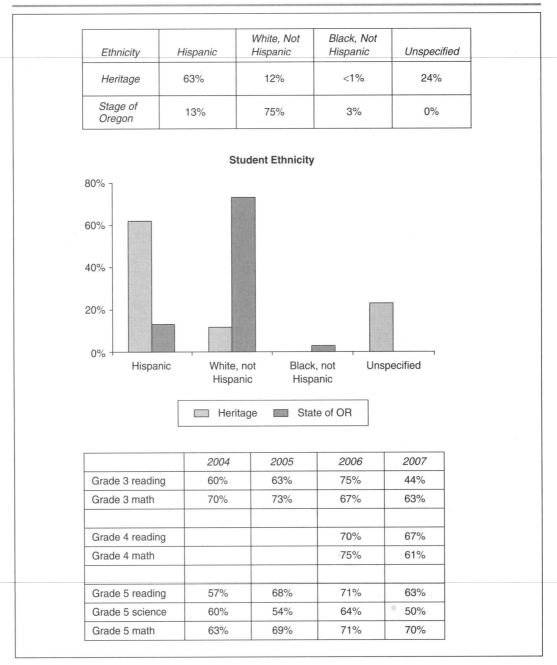

Ethnicity	Hispanic	White, Not Hispanic	Black, Not Hispanic	Unspecified
Heritage	63%	12%	<1%	24%
Stage of Oregon	13%	75%	3%	0%

Student Ethnicity

Heritage   State of OR

	2004	2005	2006	2007
Grade 3 reading	60%	63%	75%	44%
Grade 3 math	70%	73%	67%	63%
Grade 4 reading			70%	67%
Grade 4 math			75%	61%
Grade 5 reading	57%	68%	71%	63%
Grade 5 science	60%	54%	64%	50%
Grade 5 math	63%	69%	71%	70%

Note: There was a new principal in the school in 2007.

Their journey will never be complete. The challenges will continue to grow, but the professional learning community that has developed will work together to ensure that they and their students are engaged in purposeful work and meaningful learning.

IN SUMMARY

High-quality professional learning communities increase the success of their students as they engage in purposeful study and learning while developing and implementing high-yield strategies to ensure

- high-quality curriculum for every child,
- a curriculum commonly used by all teaching teams at a grade level or course of study,
- aligned assessment strategies,
- meaningful, intriguing instructional strategies, and
- extended opportunities for students to learn.

The community nurtures and cares for each member to support high-quality instruction in every classroom. They are in continuous study and reflection and convinced that their efforts directly impact the learning of each and every student. Everyone assumes responsibility for student learning and takes ownership and leadership responsibilities for achieving the school's goals for all students. The school principal and the school leadership team play an integral role in orchestrating the sometimes harmonious, sometimes cacophonous, symphony of learning.

REFLECTIVE QUESTIONS

- What are the big ideas or concepts that you are taking away from reading Chapter 1? What are the possible implications of these ideas for your team?
- What challenge strategies have you and your team used? What assumptions did you hold that facilitated collaboration and community learning? What assumptions are barriers?
- As you were reading the chapter, what celebrations are in order for your learning community?
- What are your team's greatest challenges in embedding daily conversations and professional learning about curriculum systems?
- What learning do you as a team want to do to explore these concepts deeper?
- What next steps will you take? Why? What hopes and aspirations do you have for your team if you take these steps?

EXTENDED LEARNING OPPORTUNITIES

1. Research other schools in your own district, schools inside the United States, or around the world that are very successful professional learning communities. Visit with them about the strategies that work best for them. Explore with

them how they became a professional learning community, what barriers they overcame, and how they overcame them. Ask them to share with you what barriers they are still facing and what strategies are essential for them to continue to sustain their energy and work. Reflect on this research and what everyone in the community is learning. Determine possible implications for your team and next steps. Then act!

2. Conduct a walk through in your school. Consider the vision you and your leadership team have of your professional learning community. Use this vision to establish what you will look for as you walk. What strengths did you find that connect to that vision? What challenges do you see? What surprised you? What next steps might you wish to explore? (See Resource D, A Learning Walk.)

3. Survey your staff or host focus group meetings to uncover the staff's assumptions about professional learning, about their assessments of their strengths and their challenges related to professional development, and their attitudes toward charting and establishing a long-term, sustained learning journey. Consider their responses and your possible next steps in moving your school to daily-embedded professional learning for every one.

2

Establishing Assumptions About Student and Staff Learning

I believe we can change the world if we start listening to one another again. Simple, honest, human conversation. Not mediation, negotiation, problem-solving, debate, or public meetings. Simple, truthful conversation where we each have a chance to speak, we each feel heard, and we each listen well.

—Meg Wheatley, President, Berkana Institute,
charitable leadership foundation, author,
management leadership consultant, and organizational theorist

The message is consistent and clear. Learning organizations are not content merely to describe the future they seek; they also articulate and promote the attitudes, behaviors, and commitments that must exist to create that future. Therefore, when faculty members have reached consensus on the vision of the school they are trying to create, they must then focus on reaching consensus on the shared values they intend to promote and protect.

—Rick DuFour, Founder of Solution Tree, author, and
international consultant on professional learning communities

17

What are the values that give communities new energy and open up new possibilities? What assumptions about professional learning are generative? What assumptions drain those in the organization of energy and stifle learning? The basic assumption of this book is that daily professional learning through collaboration, designing curriculum, sharing ideas, and reflecting on practice with each other facilitates learning of all students and staff.

ASSUMPTIONS

- In schools where communities of staff are learning daily from each other, students are learning.
- When teaching teams believe all students can and will learn what is essential for them to know, more students achieve.
- When communities believe that schools control the conditions that result in confident, competent learners, achievement of all students increases.
- Learning communities, rather than individual and uncoordinated efforts, are more successful with all children.
- Powerful professional learning occurs in communities as teams of teachers act intentionally on their beliefs and gently confront those assumptions that prevent them from systematically learning together.
- Authentic conversations and clarification about the community's assumptions about student and adult learning build healthy learning communities.

ASSUMPTIONS AS OPPORTUNITIES OR BARRIERS

An organization's assumptions either close or open the organization to learning (Hirsh & Killion, 2007; Sparks & Hirsh, 1997). Those organizations that hold fast to the assumption that the experts outside the school are more effective in changing the organization fail to see the possibilities and power of embedded daily community learning. Many school district central office administrators focus staff development resources on purchasing new programs, materials, and initiatives, and bringing in training to facilitate new teaching behaviors. They hold fast to the belief that school communities do not have the expertise to make these decisions. The more deeply engrained these assumptions, the less likely that those in the organization will have faith that the staff inside the school can and do have the power to change and learn as they work together daily.

Not only do many district leaders have little faith that school staff can be successful with all students, but many school staff members believe they have little control over student outcomes (Blankstein, 2004; Edmonds, 1979). A school staff's assumptions, beliefs, and values about student and staff learning either facilitate staff in leading all students to high levels of success, or their beliefs lead to the self-fulfilling prophecy that some students just cannot meet the standards, that the staff has no control over student learning, and that society and other factors are overriding the power of those in the school.

Many assumptions about professional development continue to be barriers to schools becoming professional learning communities. If school leaders believe that professional development is a program, a training session, or a speaker, they tend not to view teachers being in conversation around curriculum issues as professional learning. Some tend to "schedule" professional development after school or on weekends. Professional learning is something to be done outside the teachers' school day as an "add on" to the real work of the teacher. Furthermore, teaching teams are distracted often by the assumptions that curriculum work is a waste of time, someone else's responsibility, or done by the state. Curriculum is viewed as a stagnant, established document and not a constantly revised, living document regularly reinvented by reflecting on practice. In addition, because of the assumption that professional development is something done to them, many teachers often do not find value in professional development and reflect negative attitudes toward it. A joke that many speakers shared several years ago went something like this: A teacher died and went to heaven. When Saint Peter was showing the teacher the homes and streets where teachers lived, she noticed no one was home. She asked Saint Peter, "Where are all the teachers?" He responded, "Oh, we sent them to hell for a day of staff development." When educators hold these assumptions to be true, little involvement or ownership of professional learning occurs in the school.

Sometimes assumptions about students interfere with educators' successes with all students. An assumption that often holds educators back is an unstated belief that some students just cannot be successful in school. There are other assumptions that keep teaching teams from achieving high levels of success: assumptions about expectations of themselves and students, assumptions about the sequencing of curriculum standards, assumptions about timing and pacing of instruction, and assumptions about working together. Dennis Sparks (2007) in his book *Leading for Results* and Noel Tichy (2002) in his book *The Cycle of Leadership* both emphasize the power of assumptions and teachable points of view in facilitating change or removing barriers.

One of my favorite stories is about Southwest Airlines. Southwest Airlines has innovatively and courageously changed the airline industry (Gittell, 2003). Several years ago I came across the book *NUTS! Southwest Airlines' Crazy Recipe for Business and Personal Success* (Frieberg & Frieberg, 1998). The authors researched the positive deviance of the airline and shared the stories of its success. In a "nutshell," so they say, Southwest Airlines built a successful airline on the following "nutty" ideas:

It's nuts for a company to

- keep prices at rock bottom;
- expedite boarding by not issuing seat assignments;
- believe that customers come second;
- settle a major legal dispute by arm wrestling;
- loathe the titles and trappings of "terminal professionalism;"
- run recruiting ads that say, "Work at a place where wearing pants is optional;"
- paint its $30 million assets to look like killer whales and state flags;
- avoid TQM (total quality management), reengineering, and other trendy management programs;
- spend a lot more time planning parties than writing policies;
- avoid formal, documented strategic plans; and
- make the "Lone Ranger" leadership mentality a thing of the past. (p. 2)

The concepts were not and are not current practice even in the airline business today. The countercultural assumptions that guide Southwest Airlines seem to be that

- customers will have exceptional care and be delighted with our services if we hire the right people and take care of them;
- employees are not the primary source of cost but rather a valuable source of knowledge for reducing cost and delivering high-quality, reliable service;
- if employees have fun, customers have fun;
- high-quality work in all areas depends on leadership throughout the organization, mutual respect for all employees and their work, and a strong understanding of the entire team's interdependency; and
- through high-performance relationships of employees who share goals, knowledge, and mutual respect, Southwest will achieve low-cost, high-quality service and sustain profitability.

How did these new and different assumptions open up new possibilities for Southwest Airlines?

Through learning new assumptions, they reenvisioned airline travel and employee relationships. What are their results?

Southwest Airlines has been profitable every year from 31 years—an unsurpassed record in the highly turbulent, frequently unprofitable, airline industry. For most of 2002 the total market value of Southwest—about $9 billion—was larger than that of all other major U.S. airlines combined. The business press has celebrated Southwest in *Fortune* magazine calling it 'the most successful airline in history.' Southwest has also achieved high levels of employee satisfaction. It has been included in *Fortune* magazine's list of the 100 Best Companies to Work for in America three years in a row, and has consistently enjoyed lower turnover rants than any other U.S. airlines. (Gittell, 2002, p. 3)

Noel Tichy (2002), author of *The Cycle of Leadership*, shared the General Electric story of how the organization reinvented leadership development by developing new assumptions. The organization began its transformation to focus on the development of leaders by declaring teachable points of view (TPOV). He and Jack Welch, the former CEO of General Electric, became increasingly concerned about leadership succession. They establish the assumption that if the organization was to have sufficient frontline leadership around the world, everyone in a leadership position would need to be an aggressive learner ("Everyone learns, everyone teaches, and everyone gets smarter every day"(Tichy, 2002, p. 2). This principle guides GE to establish annually TPOV for its employees. Their leadership has guided other organizations to consider their assumptions or TPOV. Through thoughtful dialogue, sharing, and clarification, these agreed-on assumptions guide the transformation of the organizations. An engaging assumption is that the key to achievement is the leader's ability to raise the collective intelligence of the team. These leaders, clear about their assumptions, regularly share their stories and examples in ways that are intellectually clear to others and emotionally engaging for all so that all in the organization align their actions with their assumptions.

Declaring new assumptions not only opened opportunities for learning in the business world but also in education. In *Rethinking High School*, Harvey Daniels, Marilyn Bizar, and Steven Zemelman (2001) share the journey of college professors in creating the Best Practices High School in Chicago. The team decided to reshape its design based on the beliefs that high schools can be places of learning for students and staff. My favorite quote is early in the book:

> One thing we learned we can say right at the outset. We are now much, much slower to judge or criticize anyone else who works in a high school. As three college professors who enjoy the luxury of assembling fulfilling lives for ourselves out of a mixture of teaching, writing, research, and consulting, we stand in awe of people who get up every day, get in their cars, and go teach five classes of teenagers, one hundred fifty (or more) complicated souls a day, twenty or thirty years in a row, who keep believing, trusting, and laughing. Teaching adolescents is not a job for the faint of heart. This is among the hardest work in the world, and these teachers, these veterans, the ones who have stayed in touch with their idealism, who have kept reading and learning themselves, who never give up on a struggling student, these are some of the finest people in the world. (p. 9)

What an assumption to guide learning in this high school! What other assumptions did this team use to guide their design and work? Students and staff have the best opportunity for success with all students when

- the high school is small—or feels small;
- the curriculum is integrated and meaningful to students;
- every student is known, appreciated, and included in a diverse, collaborative community;
- both students and teachers exercise choice and make decisions in all elements of school life;
- teachers collaborate with students to explore and employ a growing repertoire of instructional strategies;
- with their teachers, young people engage in challenging inquiry into topics that matter;
- young people are engaged in the life of the community and the world of work;
- the school day and calendar provide flexibility and variable blocks of time for learning;
- contemporary technology and rich materials support students as thinkers, researchers, and authors;
- teachers help students to monitor, evaluate and guide their own thinking;
- teachers are students of instruction, with many opportunities to learn and grow; and
- the school works closely with parents, community organizations, and educational institutions.

What learning led them to these assumptions? What new learning did these assumptions inspire? In *Rethinking High School* (Daniels et al., 2001), the team shares their search for powerful strategies for building relationships with high school students, the kinds of curricula that intrigue high school students, and strategies for structuring learning opportunities to maximize time. They studied effective staff development strategies for embedding professional learning into the life of the school and for developing teacher leadership. Though they had the luxury of hiring the staff, they were drawing from others who had worked across the district and state. Many eager, passionate teachers hold historically, deeply embedded assumptions about high schools and how they should function. How did the development of these assumptions and making them explicit open learning opportunities for the staff? Through all their research and learning, they established the following basic principles or assumptions to guide their work:

- The central goal of schooling is intellectual development.
- Students who study a few essential areas deeply and construct meaning gain greater understandings.
- High expectations for everyone yield high results for everyone.
- When learning environments are personalized, students develop confidence as learners.
- Teachers who coach and guide students become powerful partners with them in their learning and build meaningful relationships.
- Learning of everyone, students and staff, is essential to success.
- Those who engage in democratic schools have the power to make their own decisions, determine their own solutions, and own the results of their work.

What was the result of their efforts to design a school based on new assumptions about student and staff learning—assumptions that deviate from the current assumptions grounding the practices in most highs schools across the country today? The students' performance on standardized scores went from the lowest in Chicago to the third highest in three years.

FOCUS QUESTIONS

- What assumptions do we hold as a community that facilitate our learning together? What beliefs do we have that hold us back?
- What assumptions about our students facilitate our holding high expectations for each of them? What beliefs or assumptions do we hold that create barriers to our success with every child?
- What assumptions, if we were to act as though we believed them, would yield more promising results? Which are we willing to live by purposefully, intentionally?

A VISION

As school leadership teams develop communities that learn every day, they have the greatest promise of meeting the needs of all students. Significant research (Hall & Hord, 2001) suggests the benefit of everyone in the school learning. For schools to truly implement effective professional learning in their communities, leadership in the school helps others to develop and declare guiding assumptions about professional learning and its impact on student success.

Figure 2.1   Comparing Traditional Approaches to Professional Development With the Professional Learning Community

Traditional Perspective	Professional Learning Communities
• Values and assumptions are rarely, if ever, discussed publicly. • Ungrounded assumptions about poor performance of students focus the staff's attention on the factors that impact student learning, which they have little or no control over. • Those in the school often blame those outside the school for lack of collaboration among staff or lack of adequate or effective professional development and resources. • New teachers are often inducted by experienced staff into these unspoken, unwritten, not agreed upon assumptions through coaching and mentoring—"This is just the way things are done around here! You're new; you will catch on!"	• Values are publicly debated and thoughtfully crafted to promote the learning of everyone in the organization. • The values, assumptions, or beliefs guide the design of professional learning. • Collaborative teams engage in professional learning strategies intentionally formulated to increase student performance and success in school. • Staff members are "on the lookout" for values that hinder learning of all in the organization and gently confront the issues so that these traditional, sometimes hidden values do not become barriers to learning of staff and students. • Because these values, assumptions, or beliefs are publicly agreed upon, everyone and every strategy used to increase learning are aligned with them. • Staff members who play leadership roles in the school induct new staff members into the values, assumptions, and beliefs of the organization as well as the vision and mission of the school so that expectations are clear to everyone. • Principals are learning with their teams and from other principals. They are integral to hosting focused conversations, intentionally grounding the actions of the school in the school's assumptions and questioning practices that do not seem aligned.

CHALLENGE STRATEGIES

School teams who are successful give careful consideration to designing strategies for uncovering and clarifying assumptions held in common among staff. Through structured conversations, teams develop clear statements about their assumptions, values, or beliefs about professional learning and student achievement. They begin a collective inquiry about who they are, what they value, and whether or not those values facilitate their learning and the learning of their students. They ground their conversations in the beliefs of the school community—what the community collectively thinks and how it impacts what they do. They explore together which assumptions lead teams to powerful learning for themselves and for their students. As these conversations lead the school community to deeper understandings to clarify their beliefs, they begin to question whether their assumptions are facilitating their work together or hindering the achievement of their learning. These conversations alone are powerful professional learning experiences.

1. Host a series of small group sessions for the school staff to clarify their thinking about the following questions. Make a chart that makes visible the community's assumptions. Post them so that people often reflect on them. Add or make comments for revisions that make these statements clearer.

- Who are we as a community of learners?
- What do we really believe about student learning?
- What values do we hold in common about our learning? About student learning?
- How do we learn best together?
- What values do other schools hold that allow them to be innovative, to learn together, and to ensure the success of every child?
- How can we accomplish more together than through isolated, individual efforts?
- How will we study together? How will we use our work to determine our own professional learning needs?

2. What is our vision of professional learning?

- What is our vision of how we will learn together? What will teams and individuals be doing? (You may find Resource E helpful in starting your conversations.)
- What are our greatest strengths as a community of learners? What are our greatest challenges?
- What are possible causal factors that resulted in these strengths and challenges? What are possible remedies for our challenges?
- What are essential learning strategies for us?
- What plan of action do we need?

3. What norms or "rules of the game" do we need to ensure we are learning from each other every day? Examples and possible starter norms for initiating the conversation about norms may be found in Resource F. Ask teams to consider the barriers they continuously face to working well together and to establish rules to guide their work. Rules never seem to be necessary until team members are in difficulty in their relationships and their collaborative efforts.

- As a community, articulate what problems the team seems to face when they are working together. Are there issues about people not showing up? Not showing up on time? Are there concerns about sidebar conversations and people not totally engaged? Are there issues related to members genuinely listening to each other? Does the team have trust issues? Is it difficult for members to participate out of fears related to confidentiality? Maybe the concerns are lack of follow-through?
- Whatever the issues are, the most effective teams establish a set of rules or norms around those things.

A STORY

Another compelling story is of Quakertown High School (Psencik, Czaplicki, Houston, & Kopp, 2007, pp. 14–18). Quakertown Community Senior High School in Quakertown, Pennsylvania, was no exception to the national perspective that high schools today are under performing and not meeting the needs of all of their students. In many classrooms at Quakertown High, little if any professional conversation was occurring among teachers about instructional strategies. Students were vibrant and active in the hallways; however, they were bored and not engaged in the classrooms.

While the high school had a great need for change, there was little evidence of a sense of urgency from inside the school. Most of the pressure for change was coming from outside the school from parents, community members, and central office administrative staff. Parents and community members were appearing at board meetings to complain about high taxes, high teacher salaries, and low student performance on state standardized tests. Since pressure from outside the school had had no impact on the staff's efforts to transform teaching and learning, central office administration agreed that the changes in the high school would have to emerge from the high school faculty. They held a strong assumption that if teacher leaders in the high school were inspired to examine their own practice and begin learning effective instructional practices from each other and from the research, the entire school staff would become a learning community.

To change this culture, the district's central administration initiated an effort called Best Practices in High School by selecting a few strategic faculty members and key formal and informal teacher leaders who would design, shape, and lead a new vision for the staff. The faculty had to make fundamental shifts in their beliefs and practices if student performance on standardized tests were to improve. They had resigned themselves to the fact that they had little impact on or responsibility for student learning—they were doing the best they could. Even though teams of teachers were writing curriculum based on Wiggins's (1993) concept of enduring understandings and essential questions, the work was really guided by central office staff, and teachers were struggling with the value of it in their teaching. Teachers experienced little if any significant professional conversations. They lived in a climate of isolation. They had no strategies or support in place to encourage open sharing among all staff members to talk about the issues, to analyze data, to establish a common vision, or to assist teachers in working together. As Dave Tyson, social studies lead teacher and previous district union president, put it, "We had no long term strategy for even talking about our beliefs and the strategies that we needed to learn from each other." They finally came to agree that if they studied and learned together what makes a Best Practices High School, and if they supported each other in using those strategies effectively with all students, student achievement would increase.

The leadership team began the conversations, research, and vision building. They studied *Rethinking High School* (Daniels et al., 2001) and Dennis Spark's (2002) *Designing Powerful Learning for Teachers and Principals.* They studied *Best Practices* and journal articles from many different perspectives about powerful curriculum, instruction, collaboration, culture and environment, reflection, and student responsibility. They developed their own vision and plans of action to achieve their dreams (see their work in Resource G). The leadership team began to talk openly about what they really believed about their own professional learning, and they established strategies to learn from each other.

They even began hosting those conversations with the entire high school faculty. The faculty became intrigued. They began to realize the need for all staff members to be engaged in collaboration. The leadership team researched models within successful high schools around the country that valued and used common collaboration time during the school day to increase student learning. They shared with the school board what they were learning through their Best Practices efforts and the impact of their work on student learning. They requested time for full-faculty collaboration and shared their researched plan of action. The request was unanimously approved. Now all staff members were engaged. At least once a month, school started late and all staff members were in collaborative learning communities. Sometimes, the staff used collaboration times to design model lessons. Sometimes, they shared Best Practices in their own classrooms and models of student work. They developed curriculum and assessment strategies together, and they used tuning protocols to strengthen their implementation of strategies. The whole faculty was becoming a professional learning community. They mentored and coached struggling and new teachers. They developed model classrooms for observations. They established a teacher resource room for sharing sample lessons, Best Practices instructional strategies, and powerful curriculum models of enduring understandings and essential questions.

The leadership team, working with the entire faculty, began to confront some of their most serious barriers to success. The staff honestly struggled to accept the belief or assumption that they had much control over student learning. Through continuous dialogue, study, and intense focus on what they did believe they controlled, student achievement increased. When they understood their power as a community of learners, their work resulted in increases in student learning.

Figure 2.2 Grade 11 Percentage Proficient and Advanced on the State's Assessment

	2001	2002	2003	2004	2005	2006
Math	49%	48%	51%	52%	52%	64%
Reading	58%	58%	59%	64%	71%	75%

Figure 2.3 Writing Percentage Proficient on the State's Writing Assessment

	2003	2004	2005	2006
Advanced	5%	4%	11%	30%
Proficient	57%	63%	56%	61%
Basic	20%	17%	18%	9%
Below basic	16%	15%	14%	0%

IN SUMMARY

Teams develop their assumptions over time as they learn and work together. The community of learners who begin with honest discussions about their assumptions about learning and learners opens the way to new opportunities and allows the team to challenge their own assumptions that have been barriers to them.

REFLECTIVE QUESTIONS

1. What big ideas stand out for you and your team about the power of declaring assumptions about the community's professional learning?

2. What ideas are much clearer to you and the community about the essential work of professional learning and its impact on student outcomes?

3. What assumptions have you and the community of learners established that you believe will have the greatest impact on the energy, work, and results of your professional learning?

4. How will you apply these assumptions each day with your community?

5. What celebrations are in order?

EXTENDED LEARNING OPPORTUNITIES

1. At every staff meeting or meeting of a department or grade level, ask team members to share the power of the agreed upon assumption in guiding learning of staff and students. Capture these comments in a staff journal; post them on the school Web site.

2. Establish a blog in which staff members regularly share the meaning of the assumptions in guiding their learning and their work with their students. Share the comments at staff meetings.

3. Establish a team that will walk around the school in a scavenger hunt to uncover high-quality alignment of professional learning practices with the values, assumptions, and beliefs of the organization about professional learning. Chart the findings, and share them with the staff.

4. Establish a plan of action to celebrate those powerful practices and to remove strategies that are not aligned.

5. Study the NSDC (National Staff Development Council) book *Moving NSDC Standards into Practice: Innovation Configurations* (Roy & Hord, 2003). Use the IC (innovation configurations) maps for teachers and principals under the Standards Learning, Collaboration, and Quality Teaching to ask small teams of staff to assess their strengths and weaknesses and set goals for themselves.

6. Contact NSDC about the use of the SAI (Standards Assessment Inventory) in establishing data about the school's strengths and weaknesses on all the standards to establish a school goal. As a community, use this data to set long-term, intermediate, and short-term goals for the school.

3

Determining Complex Curriculum Standards and Concepts

Curriculum design helps teachers see the connections, find resources, and make multidisciplinary curricula happen in their own classrooms. The process empowers educators to decide how and what to teach rather than allowing the curriculum to evolve accidentally. Curriculum design helps teachers see the bigger picture that students experience.

In 1860, British philosopher and sociologist Herbert Spencer asked, "What is worth knowing?" As the amount of information and the technology to access information has exploded world wide, this question remains one of the most important we ponder as educators.

—Linda Hummel Fitzharris,
"Making All the Right Connections"

Herbert Spencer's question is certainly compelling for the community of learners: "What is worth knowing?" This question challenged the just born United States early in the 1800s. Thomas Jefferson responded with the belief that grounded the young democracy in the value of education for its citizens. Jefferson stated that only through an educated and liberated citizenry with civic concerns, not just religious ones, could the young country survive as a democracy.

In 1918, the National Education Association (NEA) Commission on Reorganization of Secondary Education published the famous "Cardinal Principles for Secondary Education." The commission noted that:

- the seven major aims of the Cardinal Principles should compose education; they are health, command of the fundamentals, worthy home membership, vocation, citizenship, leisure, and ethical character;
- high schools should be comprehensive institutions based on the various social and economic groups that populate the nation; and
- high school curricula should offer various programs to meet various needs of students—agricultural, business and commercial, vocational, and college preparatory.

The quest for the answer to the question, What is worth knowing? is continued today by national and educational leaders and researchers. Education communities who grapple with the question's many challenging possible answers learn together as they continuously design and redesign the curriculum. Through their efforts, they ensure that the nation's youth are ready, skilled, and competent. These courageous teaching teams begin to question their own outcomes for their classes, their assessment strategies, and their instructional practices. They ensure that their instruction is focused and purposeful every day, and students are clear about what they are to learn.

In some ways, educators are both assisted and challenged by the tremendous number of resources from national teacher organizations, state departments of education, and state and national workforce developing communities. International baccalaureate, college boards, and a plethora of authors and book publishers who write on the subject are all confident that they have the answer to the very complex question, what is worth knowing?

ASSUMPTIONS

Communities who learn together and increase the success of all students

1. are continuously struggling with and clarifying what is worth knowing,
2. study the needs of their students from the world's viewpoints and perspectives,
3. analyze their research and thinking to establish powerful student-performance expectations in their school or in their discipline,
4. clarify these student-performance expectations by developing complex content standards for their courses of study or grade levels, and
5. ground their complex content standards for themselves and their students by discerning the undergirding principles, concepts, and theories that make those standards essential learning.

WHAT ARE COMPLEX CONTENT STANDARDS?

Grant Wiggins and Jay McTighe (1998) define complex standards as standards or skills that students must apply in their schoolwork. These standards expect students to design systems that solve problems, create new ideas, and matter to themselves and others beyond the school. The first aspect of the definition seems direct enough. Complex standards expect students to use what they are learning in some new way. For example, students are expected to use their skills in writing to share articulately and clearly who they are and what they are learning. They write to make their points so compelling that readers are intrigued. They write for fun and use a variety of forms such as poetry, drama, or letter writing to express themselves. Students use scientific-inquiry processes to explore their world and establish hypotheses for themselves. They skillfully analyze data so that they may draw logical conclusions. Students uncover historical discourses and multiple, conflicting perspectives to make sense of the world and formulate interventions to keep history from repeating itself.

The second aspect of Wiggins and McTighe's (1998) definition is much more challenging. Complex curriculum expects students to design systems—systems for problem solving, systems for designing systems, systems for exploring their world, systems for study and reflection. When students design systems, they are organize their thinking to create a process to achieve a goal or produce a product. When designing systems, students think differently about their work. They try to figure out how they might accomplish their goals together. They communicate with others by posing new ideas, making predictions, and solving problems. They might have conversations like these:

> If we are going to really drop this egg from the top of our fire department's truck and do not want it broken when it lands, what will we need to do to protect it? What mathematical reasoning would help us anticipate the impact of the fall? What design might be the best to ensure its safety? What materials might we use? What will we do first? Second? How might it look?
>
> If we are going to explore water quality in our community's river, what do we mean by *water quality*? What are the standards that indicate water quality? What tools are used in the profession to make these judgments? How are we going to explore this together? What kind of data do we need to collect? What are the best ways to collect that data? How often do we need to collect it? What will we need to do first? Second? How will we report and display our findings so that others will understand? How do the experts do this work? How will we determine our recommendations?

That is systems thinking!

The third criterion in Wiggins and McTighe's (1998) definition is that the students must find value in their work and what they are learning and apply it outside the school. This challenge may be the greatest. How do educators help students make connections through real-world experiences? What are real-world experiences? Some approaches may be as simple as students working together to design a community garden. They use their geometry skills to design the plot of land for the garden. They use the knowledge and skills of soil physics, plant growth, and seasons to determine the planting and care of the garden. They determine strategies for engaging the community in the work and distributing food to those who need it the most. Another example might be students using their language arts skills to interview World War II veterans to produce a book of their life stories that they will publish and place in their school and community libraries.

WHAT ARE THE STANDARDS ESSENTIAL FOR STUDENTS TO BE SUCCESSFUL IN THE WORLD?

The 21st Century Workforce Commission's (2000) National Alliance of Business established the following framework for complex curriculum:

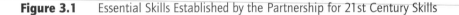

Figure 3.1   Essential Skills Established by the Partnership for 21st Century Skills

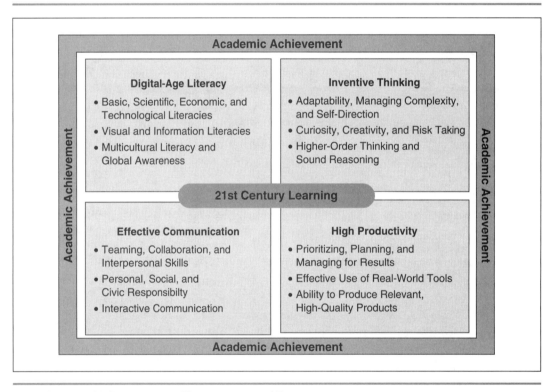

Source: The Partnership for 21st Century Skills, www.21stcenturyskills.org.

As teaching teams grapple with and respond honestly to this essential question, what is worth knowing? they begin to rethink what is worth knowing, and they purposefully design instruction. The failure to explore the question honestly often leaves teaching teams unclear about what students are to learn. They tend to follow the text. They are often frustrated about the amount of curriculum to be covered. The district and school leadership, concerned about school ratings, may even send the message, "What is worth knowing is what is tested." The lack of conversation among teaching teams about what students are to know often results in students believing that nothing in school will help them in the world in which they live. Too many students believe school is boring and that their work is not about putting forth effort or learning but completing tasks and assignments.

The second major conversation to respond to the question, what is worth knowing? is to consider the big ideas, principles, or concepts that undergird the standards. What are concepts? In her book, *Concept-Based Curriculum and Instruction*, Erickson (2002) defines a concept as a principle or rule, a big idea that is a result of observations made in the world. For example, as we observe the time of sunrise and sunset over time, we uncover or discover some predictable rules about the times of sunsets and sunrises throughout the year. As we observe sufficient characteristics of a certain writer, we begin to make judgments about the characteristics of that writer.

Wiggins and McTighe (1998) have also focused on concepts, or what they call "enduring understandings," as essential to curriculum concerns for teachers. They challenge teaching teams to consider, "What are the big ideas with enduring value beyond the classroom? What is at the heart of the discipline?"(p. 10–11).

Understanding at a conceptual level helps learners make connections, make predictions, accelerate their learning, and find deeper meaning in their work. Through their own observations of the world, learners construct their own knowledge and understandings. If students have an understanding of the causes of war, they accelerate their analysis of all wars because they have discovered common threads. If students deeply understand that all writers use similar processes for writing, they are more likely to apply those processes to their own work. When students develop conceptual understanding, they develop purposeful, strategic meaning to what they are learning. This application accelerates student learning and strengthens the possibility that students will produce greater-quality work. After working with the ideas of concepts with her teaching team, a Grade 12 high school Language Arts teacher decided to share the concepts with her class by having them respond to them in writing. One of her students responded, "After thirteen years of schooling, I finally have a big idea!" We certainly do not want any student to leave school after thirteen years without at least one big idea!

FOCUS QUESTIONS

- What is it we really want our students to know and do well?
- What are the big ideas or undergirding principles, theories, or concepts that will deepen their understanding, assist them in making connections, and accelerate their learning?

A VISION

Teaching teams host regular conversations to discuss the focus questions and to search out their own answers. They research the world in which they live, the careers of today and tomorrow, and the challenges faced by the community, the nation, and the world. They begin to define the standards and the concepts essential for the success of their students. Effective teaching teams do not isolate themselves in school but view themselves as having the greatest impact on the future lives of their students and hope for tomorrow. They regularly seek others in other fields such as technology, medicine, science, art, health, government, and economics to develop a clear picture of the needs of their students. They analyze the state and national curriculum documents available to them, and they are cautious of those who have "the answer" or "quick fixes."

Through their study and research, teaching teams declare what is worthy and essential for their students to know and do well. Knowing that the world is continuously and exponentially changing in all facets of life, they regularly revisit the question, What is worth knowing?

Principals and school-based administrators, knowing the importance of their conversations, exploration, and work, ensure adequate time in the school, facilitate connections for teachers with parents and community leaders, and provide process facilitation as needed.

Figure 3.2   Comparing Traditional Approaches to Professional Development With the Professional Learning Community

Traditional Perspective	Professional Learning Communities
• Teachers work individually to address the skills required by the state curriculum. • They follow instructional ideas and suggested strategies recommended in textbooks or materials to be used for instruction. • Though they may share with their students the essential understandings of their discipline, they often have not thought about them intentionally, and so students miss the big idea. • They assign work that is void of meaning or interest to students. • They talk often about poor-quality work and unmotivated students.	• Teaching teams work together to research the world and to combine what is essential for students to learn from their state's perspective and what is essential for their students to know to be successful beyond school. • They declare together the undergirding principles or concepts that are to be understood that will accelerate the learning of students, help them find meaning and purpose in what they are learning, and help them make connections across disciplines and within the standards they are to learn for their course of study. • They use these concepts to establish essential questions that might intrigue their students. • These teaching teams regularly reevaluate their decisions as they continuously study and learn. • Together, they use these defined standards and concepts in helping students and parents understand what is essential to know.

CHALLENGE STRATEGIES

As teaching teams in the learning community begin this lifelong journey, they authentically, genuinely explore what is worthy for students to know and do well. As they become greater and greater observers of the world, they host regular conversations about what is essential to know.

1. As a teaching team, begin with a fundamental question, What is the world really like? Use current articles, books such as *The World Is Flat* (Friedman, 2005), and publications by workforce development and scientific journals to develop deeper understandings of the complex issues that your students will be addressing as they enter the world of work of their generations.

- What are we learning in the fields of science and medicine that impacts the lives of our students?
- What about science and technology?
- What are the major political issues that will impact the future of our children? The developments of India and China, the Middle East?
- They study their state and national standards carefully.

2. Establish statements of student-performance expectations for your school, grade level, or course of study. The following is a structure and an example that might be useful to guide the conversation and develop aligned statements:

Figure 3.3   Establishing Student-Performance Expectations

Students in Our Middle School Today Will Graduate From High School in 2017.		
The world in which they will live is characterized by	*Our students, to be successful,*	
a flourishing use of technology in all careers;	must be flexible and adaptive users of technology who	value learning and are always considering and searching for new ways to use technology to produce high-quality work, easily adapt to new strategies and new ideas, and are persistent and seek alternative pathways to solve problems.
fast-paced innovation and a creative environment;	must develop deep conceptual understanding of all disciplines as well as proficiency in applying what they are learning; must be skilled at designing systems for solving real-world problems; must value what they are learning as useful to them outside of school;	

(Continued)

Figure 3.3 (Continued)

	Students in Our Middle School Today Will Graduate From High School in 2017.	
	these are students who	learn aggressively;
		understand the concepts of the scientific, mathematical, political, economic, and social worlds;
		make connections between what they are learning in school and the world around them;
		develop powerful systems for solving problems; and
		use their language skills to share what they are learning with others, develop deeper understandings, and communicate effectively; and
		are resilient, optimistic, and take setbacks as temporary.
culturally diverse world communities with varying and often conflicting, political, social, and religious perspectives.	must understand the political, cultural, and religious perspectives of the world's people so that they may	show empathy towards others;
		know who they are and what they value, while respecting other perspectives;
		resolve conflicts in nonviolent ways;
		work collaboratively;
		build consensus; and
		capitalize on the talents of all individuals regardless of their perspectives.

3. As a team, engage in the analysis of the state curriculum. Such work ensures that everyone has a deep understanding of the state content standards, the rationale used by the state to support those standards, and the emphasis the state places on certain standards that are measured on the state assessments. Analyze the standards established by national teaching organizations, such as the National Council of Teacher of Mathematics, to make comparisons and look for omissions often made by state curriculum documents. The question is still, **What is worth knowing?**

4. To begin to develop deeper understandings, develop a vision of curriculum combining research and thinking about the world and the essential learnings in the state content standards. The following chart might assist the team in structuring this conversation.

5. Discuss, what are the undergirding principles? What are the essential understandings? The sentence starter to guide the conversation is, "If students are going to communicate effectively, they must understand that. . . ."

Figure 3.4   Expanding State Content Standards to Incorporate Standards "Worth Knowing!"

Essential Content Standards Unique to Our Discipline	Work Ethics and Quality-Work Standards	Communication and Collaboration Standards	Character and Integrity Standards

Examples:

- If students are going to work effectively with others, they must understand that
  - effective teams work toward achieving a common goal and build consensus for the plan they are going to implement, and
  - effective teams listen to one another and try to see through others' points of view.
- If students are going to describe the life cycle of a butterfly, they must understand that
  - all living things have a life cycle that begins with birth and ends with death.

6. Finally, prepare a document to share with students, parents, and community members that declares what the expectations are for the content area, the course of study, or the grade level (see Resource H, Example Letter to Parents).

A STORY

Teaching teams in Petal, Mississippi, have challenged themselves to develop conceptual understanding in their students. Petal is a small community outside of Hattiesburg, Mississippi. They have approximately 3,600 students K–12 in four schools. Approximately 60% of the students receive free and reduced lunch. The social studies department K–12 discovered, in their analysis of their state standards, that almost the entire social studies curriculum is conceptual. Students had to understand that citizens in a democracy had certain rights and responsibilities. They had to understand that different branches of government had different purposes. They had to understand how geography impacted economic opportunities.

Although they could see that their curriculum was not particularly skills based, they were concerned about their state's assessments. They were not sure that helping students develop conceptual understandings would positively impact their students' performance on standardized tests; they were even concerned that their scores would drop. Because they are one of the highest-achieving school districts in the state of Mississippi on their state standardized tests, their concern was genuine. A few years ago, they were the only district in the state to reach its highest academic achievement standard (Level 5). During their ten-year journey of clarifying their curriculum, the social studies high school teaching team discovered that their scores on standardized tests were going up as they all focused on the conceptual thinking of their students. In 2006, Petal students were second in the state in performance on their state high school standardized social studies test—second only to the state's magnet high school program. The district leadership compared their top students in high school social studies and the performance of students in a state magnet program, and Petal's top students outperformed them. Teachers and administrators all attribute their students' success to their intense focus on K–12 concept-based curricula.

The following examples come from the concepts developed by teaching teams from language arts, mathematics, science, and social studies in Petal Schools, Petal, Mississippi (revised 2007).

- Language is a primary tool for exchanging and interpreting ideas in order to communicate clearly and effectively in formal and informal situations.
- Producing effective, written communication empowers authors and intrigues audiences.
- Algebra is a system allowing individuals to formulate, explain, and generalize a variety of patterns and relationships in relevant situations.
- Data and probability analysis allow individuals to collect, organize, interpret, and make inferences about information.
- Scientific inquiry enables individuals to make informed decisions related to health, ecological, and global issues.
- The validity of scientific claims is determined by gathering data based on systematic observations and measurements of a phenomenon.
- Through the study of the historical development of past cultures, we can understand and evaluate exchanges that occurred through conflict, economics, and social interactions that pave the way for the future.
- The geographic world is in a continuous state of cultural, economic, physical, and political change as seen through the study of human environment interaction, movement, place, region, and location.

IN SUMMARY

Exploring what is worth knowing is one of the fundamental questions of education. As teams explore this question together, they grow more focused and intentional in their work as a team and their work with students. There are two aspects of the question. In what skills, attitudes, and behaviors must students be proficient in order to maneuver successfully in the world around them? And what deep understandings, big ideas, and principles must they know that accelerate learning, facilitate students making essential connections, and finding value in their learning?

REFLECTIVE QUESTIONS

1. What truly resonates with you and your team in reading the ideas in this chapter and in the challenge strategies that you implemented?

2. What did you learn about your curriculum's strengths and challenges in meeting the needs of your students?

3. What new ideas emerge for you and the team?

4. What possible implications are there for you and your team?

5. What next steps might you wish to take to explore this idea further?

EXTENDED LEARNING OPPORTUNITIES

1. Spend a day once a month in a different field observing others at work and reflect with them about the skills essential for them to be successful. Often, local businesses that participate in Adopt-a-School efforts will gladly provide substitutes as a resource for teachers wishing to spend a day in the business, scientific, or technological worlds. If not, build these opportunities into the school budget and calendar. Some teaching teams have often found summer opportunities to work in the content field as a teacher in residence.

2. Visit the local workforce development board about the concerns and issues they are facing.

3. Explore what types of careers are most prevalent and the requirements essential for students to be successful in those careers.

4. Visit with those who teach college freshmen. Discuss with them their expectations.

4

Mapping the Curriculum

If improving student learning and student achievement are the goals of our schools, then it is imperative that we examine the processes that influence those goals. Specifically, we must examine how educators plan and implement curriculum and instruction.

—Susan Udelhofen, *Keys to Curriculum Mapping*

Curriculum maps are valuable documents in and of themselves, but the process for creating and discussing the maps is of equal value. In effective schools, the community learns through the processes of designing maps through their collaboration, reflective inquiry, shared purpose, and the design of curriculum coherence.

Several months ago, a friend of mine was explaining exactly why he did not want to purchase a navigational system for his car. He said he did not want to rely on such an instrument. "People need to know their way around—they need to have a strong sense of direction in their heads." I was humored because shortly after I moved from Austin to Houston, Texas, I purchased a car with a navigational system. I was extremely lost in Houston. For one thing, I believed Houston to be south of Austin—a fatal error in my sense of direction. Austin is actually due west of Houston. North and south were east and west to me. This misguided sense of direction embedded in my vision of the city hampered my navigation and resulted in my wandering around many times. Now with a computerized voice and a map that I can see easily, I am beginning to get the lay of the land! There are still challenges. I have to keep the navigational CD current. The CD certainly does not have the most current road changes or construction detours in Houston, which still are barriers to my knowing my way around. But the navigational system keeps me knowing where

I am, where I am going, and what possible alternative routes are available. An interesting point to me is that as I use the system, I am learning more and more about the city: I know when I am going west or east; I am developing my own internal navigational system to many places in the city without using the system; I am learning about Houston by using a map.

I share this story because I am confident all teaching teams need purposeful, well-thought-out, standards-driven, concept-based maps to keep them focused on the standards, to guide their design of assessments and instruction through the year, and to learn more deeply the meaning of their own standards. They learn new ways of helping students develop a conceptual understanding of their content. They are also more thoughtful about the use of classroom instructional time. Although detours and roadblocks to student learning occur all the time, maps help teaching teams keep the vision of where they are going clear in their minds and the minds of their students.

When working with the challenge strategies in Chapter 3, teaching teams expand their thinking about standards and declare their common student-performance expectations that will drive all curriculum and instruction work. The teams consider what students must do well to be good citizens, to develop workforce readiness skills, and to develop an understanding of the world in which they live. Now, the challenge is for the team to design a year that leads students to proficiency in those expectations and deepens their understanding of those concepts.

The overarching questions to guide the community's learning now are:

- How can we target the content standards to ensure proficiency and build confident, competent learners?
- How can we effectively launch and sequence these standards throughout the school year so that they grow in complexity and are coherent from unit to unit?
- How can we maximize time to immerse students in standards and revisit them sufficiently to ensure student learning?

ASSUMPTIONS

- Communities that map their curriculum standards and concepts have a navigational system that allows them to
  - focus their work for the entire school year to build proficiency in the course or grade-level student-performance expectations and to develop deep understanding of the concepts;
  - target content standards essential for supporting student mastery of the course or grade-level student-performance expectations and concepts;
  - deeply understand these targeted standards and analyze how they grow in complexity over time;
  - consider ensuring sufficient time for students to truly master a standard, develop proficiency in a skill, or deeply understand a concept; and
  - discover coherence in their curriculum.
- Curriculum maps are under continuous redesign as teams reflect on their use in designing common assessments and instruction and as they observe the learning of their students.

MAPPING THE CURRICULUM

Most everyone agrees that in the United States curriculum experts have expanded the definition of curriculum to mean many things to many people. In addition, what students are expected to learn well is overwhelming to most classroom teachers (Ainsworth, 2003; English & Steffy 2001; Schmoker, 2006). Consequently, many districts and teachers have chosen textbooks to substitute for the rigor and time required for curriculum-mapping conversations to occur. There may even be a national perspective that teachers just do not have the time or expertise to analyze their curriculum and make effective curriculum decisions. A new public school administrator shared her perspective with me: "I have just grown to believe that new teachers have too much on their minds; they are overwhelmed with simple things, such as classroom management. They just need a book to tell them what to do when it comes to curriculum issues." This perspective is contradictory to teachers becoming reflective practitioners who make research-based, data-driven decisions about curriculum, instruction, and assessment of student learning.

The greatest challenges seem to be for teaching teams to move away from the content of their discipline. Several years ago, a young social studies teacher explained to me that he had a great deal of difficulty teaching social studies today because history just keeps getting longer and longer! "We have so much stuff to cover!" The stuff is content. Students have many experiences with content, but few opportunities to explore the curriculum in depth to develop conceptual understanding and sufficient proficiency in the essential standards. Many teachers refer to the curriculum as "a mile wide and an inch deep." In the book, *The Teaching Gap* (Stigler & Hiebert, 1999), videotapes of U.S. teachers of mathematics revealed that even after extensive training and sufficient materials and many manipulatives in the classroom, teachers tend to assign problems, go over them quickly, and assign more problems. Students spend little time in discussion on a particular problem and the multiple ways the problem might be solved. They have little conversation about the mathematical reasoning that undergirds the solving of that problem. The curriculum still remains content driven and activity based.

Consequently, there is a national effort to focus on standards so that students develop essential proficiencies. Several authors and researchers discuss strategies for targeting the curriculum standards (Ainsworth, 2003; Schmoker, 2006) but few address the absolutely essential need to sequence the launching of the standards over time. Heidi Hayes Jacobs (2004) has worked hard to emphasize the need for curriculum mapping. However, without thoughtful analysis of the standards and concepts, the predominant design of curriculum maps is often content mapping and/or diary mapping, both of which are ineffective in increasing students' achievement of standards and developing students' understanding of the undergirding principles or concepts.

Content maps list topics teaching teams are going to address instructionally at a particular time. For example, a language arts team might develop a content map that lists when the teachers will teach drama or nonfiction to students, or when they will teach parts of speech. Science teachers developing a content map might list when they will teach about cells, rocks, or body systems. Since there are no verbs on these maps to define the essential student performance expected, they do not give guidance to teachers for either instruction or assessment of standards. The connections to the content standards are unclear. There is a distinct difference in identifying body systems and explaining how all the body's systems interact.

Diary maps are individual teacher maps describing the diary of a teacher's actual work. They may be content and standards driven; however, they do not reflect the thinking of planning ahead by a team of teachers. Some districts' curriculum leaders actually start the process with diary mapping. Some expect teachers to diary map after common curriculum maps are developed. Both of these practices waste precious time and often build frustration. Teachers spend inordinate amounts of time on tools they will not use in the future or will defend when working toward a consensus map. Furthermore, because these maps are often content maps, teachers are often discouraged as they continue to uncover the immense amount of content in any discipline and continue to feel the pressure to teach it all.

Sometimes, maps are produced by small teams at district levels or purchased from organizations that develop curriculum materials. These tools can certainly be of assistance to teams analyzing their content standards. However, unless teams of teachers engage in their own discovery and revise the maps based on their thinking, these tools are of little use to the teaching team and are often ignored in designing instruction and assessment strategies. No real community learning has occurred.

The most effective learning strategy for designing standards-driven, concept-based curriculum maps is for teams of teachers to use blank paper, state and national standards, scissors or computers, and collaboration. They focus on standards to begin their work. Because they are working together, they build a consensus map naturally. In addition, the standards develop new meaning to the team as they share and debate how these standards really look when students are doing them well, what the natural sequence would be, and how their curriculum standards can flow throughout the year with a natural coherence. Furthermore, it is impossible for a group of teachers who are mapping standards to not share strategies they would use to teach them. The learning occurs as teams engage in conversations. These focused conversations lead teams to develop deeper understanding of their standards and concepts and to generate great ideas for teaching them well.

FOCUS QUESTIONS

- What are the essential, targeted content standards that lead students to achieve the team's student-performance expectations? What new concepts are emerging that support these standards and skills?
- How do we best sequence these standards and concepts to ensure our students learn them well?
- What content will we use to interest the students and teach them what is essential for them to know?

A VISION

Through their own research, the principals and the school-leadership team lead the faculty to understand the value of curriculum mapping. They assist teams in designing an effective system for mapping the standards. Through the school planning process, the leadership team structures the schedule and builds in ample time and resources for teams to work together. Principals build in regularly scheduled full-day, summer work, and part-day times for intensive collaboration to design the annual map. Most of this deep thinking takes more time than what is usually allocated for daily, common planning time. Often, the full days follow marking or grade reporting times in the calendar so that teams can reflect on the impact of their work on student learning and make revisions to their map. Principals may also hire a facilitator or use a resource person from the central office or a teacher from another school to facilitate teams as they begin their work to ensure a great start. The principal and the school-leadership team continuously monitor the progress of the community, structure sharing time among teams, and celebrate efforts and learnings.

Grade-level or course-content teams make a commitment to work toward consensus on a common curriculum map that they will use to guide their instruction. They commit to developing a standards-driven, concept-based curriculum map that will be the basis for their design of common assessments and common units of study. They value their work together because they know they will capitalize on the ideas, thinking, and talents of everyone on the team.

- They revisit their student-performance expectations and course or grade-level concepts.
- The team begins the career work of analyzing their state and national standards and targeting those that are essential for students to know to become proficient in their student-performance expectations.
- They may add standards to fill in curriculum gaps that become evident to them. They may delete standards that do not ensure coherence in their curriculum.
- They may rewrite and revise standards that are not challenging enough for their students.
- Once they have confidence in their targeted standards, they decide on a format for their curriculum map that will be useful to them.
- Then, they begin the challenging task of determining the best sequence for launching standards and concepts. They may cut up state and national standards curriculum documents and begin to move them around their map to test multiple ways of thinking about the standards.
- They may also modify a curriculum map they discovered through their research.
- They target essential standards that they believe have the greatest impact on student learning.
- They consider how standards grow in complexity over time.
- Their primary question is, how can we make these standards flow throughout the year so that students make sense of them and develop proficiency?

Figure 4.1   Comparing Traditional Approaches to Professional Development With the Professional Learning Community

Traditional Perspectives	Professional Learning Communities
• Teachers are provided copies of the state standards and the textbook materials available to them and asked to be sure that	• Principals and the school leadership team facilitate the community developing a vision of the power of curriculum mapping. They value what the work teams are doing and see it as integral to the success of every student. They are continuously highlighting and celebrating the team's work and new learnings, removing barriers, and providing essential resources.

(Continued)

Figure 4.1 (Continued)

Traditional Perspectives	Professional Learning Communities
students perform successfully on these standards on the state assessments. • Teachers often follow the time allocations and curriculum maps or scope and sequences of textbook publishers. • Teachers may design curriculum maps and lessons together, but they often begin with content. • They match lessons to standards without consideration of deep, thoughtful immersions into the learning experience. • Collaboration time is often spent discussing student behavior.	• Teaching teams analyze their student-performance expectations, their course concepts, and their state standards to target the essential state content standards. • Teaching teams design a common curriculum map based on the concepts and standards they have targeted as essential for students to know and do well. • The team designs the map after thoughtful conversations about the most logical and coherent sequence of standards. They consider the recursive nature of learning and revisit standards so that students have distributed practice. • They discuss ensuring adequate time for immersions so that students develop proficiency. • As they use the map to guide the design of assessment strategies and of each unit of instruction, they reflect on the impact of their work on student learning. They make revisions to their work, and they determine what they need to investigate and learn together to address persistent challenges that they are facing. • They view the map as not only a learning experience in itself, as they share their ideas and their thinking, but also as an opportunity to identify what they do not know and what they need to learn.

CHALLENGE STRATEGIES

1. As a team of teachers who teach the same grade level or content area, establish common agreements concerning curriculum design for the team. For example:

- Will we honestly incorporate our school, grade level, and course of study's student-performance expectations and concepts onto our curriculum map?
- Will we work together to develop a powerful curriculum map that will guide our design of assessment and instruction?
- Will we honestly consider the complexity of our curriculum and ensure the work we do gives students the best opportunity to learn these skills, attitudes, and behaviors well?
- Will we agree on a common format for our map and ensure that it is our best thinking about how to launch our standards?
- Will we commit to each other to regularly review the value of the map in guiding our work, the value of our map in increasing student learning, and make necessary changes in our work?
- Will we use our work to determine our professional learning needs?

2. Determine a plan of action for developing a common curriculum map. Review the work on analyzing the needs of students, the newly established student-performance expectations, and the state's content standards. Remember that the essential question is, what is worth knowing?

3. Establish a process for targeting essential standards. Some state content standards are repeated over and over and can be combined. Some are nice to know but not essential to developing proficiency in students. Some teams, afraid to omit any state content standards, will organize all of the standards in their state's documents into one of three categories: essential to know, important, and worthy. These teams ensure that the essential to know are on their maps and are the main focus of their assessment and instructional designs.

4. Think deeply about the sequence, timing, and launching of standards and how these decisions impact student proficiency. Consider cutting and pasting curriculum documents or using computers and projectors for flexibility in moving standards around. Debate the sequence. Make predictions about student learning based on proposed sequences. Be sure to include in the essential to know category and those standards tested on the state's tests, Advanced Placement, or International Baccalaureate exams. Make sure students have been thoroughly immersed in their tested standards prior to state assessments.

5. Develop a format for the map that is user friendly to everyone on the team. Consider the following examples as they may be helpful to those who wish to develop interdisciplinary units of K–12 study or who teach in elementary school and are responsible for more than one content discipline. The following examples are designs frequently used by teaching teams. Consider these examples as starting places for designing your own format.

Figure 4.2 Curriculum Map (Example)

Unit 1: Exploring Our Political World (An Interdisciplinary Unit—Six Weeks)
Essential Questions:

Student Performance Expectations and Course-/Grade-Level Concepts	Standards/ Benchmarks *State-Tested Benchmark	Concepts (Enduring Understandings)	Content	Essential Materials/ Alignment to Text	Notes
	Reading Writing Mathematics Science Social Studies Work force readiness Technology literacy				
Culminating Assessments Scoring Tools (Rubrics)					

(Continued)

Figure 4.2 (Continued)

Unit 2: Exploring the Scientific World (Six Weeks)
Essential Questions:

Student Performance Expectations and Course-/Grade-Level Concepts	Standards/ Benchmarks *State-Tested Benchmark	Concepts (Enduring Understandings)	Content	Essential Materials/ Alignment to Text	Notes

Culminating Assessments
Scoring Tools (Rubrics)

Another format used is actually a horizontal view of the exact same elements. Some teaching teams prefer to look across the year—after all it is a map. (See Figure 4.3)

The key elements of a standards-driven, concept-based map are student-performance expectations, course-/grade-level essential or targeted content standards, concepts, content, and time allocation. Optional elements deemed useful by some teams are identification of aligned materials, assessment strategies, and notes for reflection.

Figure 4.4 is an actual map used by the Valor staff:

1. When developing interdisciplinary units of study, start working with the standards from one content area, and map the entire content area targeted standards before making connections to another content area. Elementary teams may choose either science or socials studies standards for their beginning focus because of the interests or needs of students. Those teaching teams, who have only one content area, map their targeted content standards. The team then searches other content standards from other disciplines and selects and highlights natural connections to their content standards. For example, secondary teachers who teach courses in mathematics, when working with data analysis, probability, and statistics content standards, may find natural connections to standards in science and language arts. Make the connections evident on the map.

Figure 4.3   Example Format for a Curriculum Map

Student Performance Expectations and Course-/Grade-Level Concepts			
	Unit 1: Exploring Our Political World— First Trimester	Unit 2: Exploring the Scientific World— Second Trimester	Unit 3: Third Trimester
Standards			
Concepts			
Content			
Essential materials			
Culminating assessments			
Scoring rubrics			

Figure 4.4   Valor Middle School

Grade 8 Social Studies Yearlong Plan

Student Performance Expectations	Unit 1: Civics and Government Dates: Sept. 5 to Dec. 1	Unit 2: Reconstruction and Westward Migration Dates: Dec. to Mar. 15	Unit 3: Industrialization and Globalization Dates: Mar. 19 to Jun. 14
All students communicate using reading, writing, and speaking modes.	Concepts: Citizens in a democracy have rights and responsibilities for themselves and others.	Concepts: Through the migration of people multiple cultures emerged and clashed.	Concepts: The demand for products impacts the supply.

(Continued)

Figure 4.4 (Continued)

Student Performance Expectations	Unit 1: Civics and Government Dates: Sept. 5 to Dec. 1	Unit 2: Reconstruction and Westward Migration Dates: Dec. to Mar. 15	Unit 3: Industrialization and Globalization Dates: Mar. 19 to Jun. 14
All students use strategies that help them increase their comprehension in all stages of reading, in both fiction and non-fiction.	The Constitution determines how the government is shaped and it is the responsibility of the people to know it and uphold it.	With the challenges of migration and westward movement came great creativity. The physical geography helps determine available resources and culture.	Invention precedes demand, yet demand inspires invention. Educational and intellectual power of a country determines its healthy future.
All students understand and appreciate human value, diversity, and interactions, both social and environmental. All students investigate topics of interest and importance. They will select appropriate media sources, use effective research processes, and demonstrate ethical use of resources and materials. (Copyright, citation, etc.) All students demonstrate knowledge of spelling, grammar, punctuation, capitalization, and penmanship. All students understand, learn, and use new vocabulary discovered through their readings of informational text and literary text.	Standards: Explain citizens' rights and how the Constitution protects those rights. - *Identify the rights of citizens.* - *Bill of Rights* - Student Handbook of Rights and Responsibilities - Due Process Share how citizens can make their voices heard in the political process. - *Identify and give examples of ways that citizens can let their opinions be known in the political process.* - *Power* - *Identify and give examples of how groups and organization can influence the actions of government.* - *Campaigns* Identify and give examples of how groups and organizations can influence the actions of government. - *Give examples.*	People influence and shape history over time. Standards: Describe how individuals, issues, and events changed or significantly influenced the course of U.S. history post–American Revolution through 1900: *Lewis and Clark expedition, westward migration, Manifest Destiny, European immigration, rural to urban migration on indigenous populations, Africans/African Americans, abolitionists, Civil War, Irish potato famine, the effects of Indian Wars and the opening of the West on Native American tribes.* Explain how various groups of people were affected by events and developments in Oregon state history: *Identify events, groups and people in the history of Oregon.*	Standards: Describe and explain how and why people respond predictably to positive and negative incentives. Describe how supply and demand responds predictably to circumstances. Explain how a wage or salary is the price of labor: *supply and demand.* Share how workers increase productivity: *skills, tools, machinery income, education and training.* Share how actions of the U.S. government affect its own citizens and those of other countries. Compare and contrast various forms of government. Explain and give examples of how the United States economy

Student Performance Expectations	Unit 1: Civics and Government Dates: Sept. 5 to Dec. 1	Unit 2: Reconstruction and Westward Migration Dates: Dec. to Mar. 15	Unit 3: Industrialization and Globalization Dates: Mar. 19 to Jun. 14
	Explain the purposes of government in the U.S. - Distinguish the purposes of government as stated in the Preamble. - Describe how the power of government is limited in the U.S. - *Describe the provision of the Bill of Rights (Amendments 1–10) that protects individual's rights.* Justify the relationship between local, state, and federal government. - *Identify the power and/or responsibility of each level of government.* - *Explain how laws are made and enforced at each level.* Describe the powers of each branch of government. - *Explain the basic idea of checks and balances.* - *Identify the legislative, executive, and judicial institutions.* **Content:** - Personal responsibilities - Civil rights - Constitution *Preamble *Bill of Rights - Presidential Elections	Describe and use fundamental geography vocabulary and concepts. - *Terms: latitude, longitude, interdependence, and accessibility.* - *Use: maps, charts, and graphs to analyze distribution, connections, distance and spatial patterns.* In the U.S. identify and/or locate: - *Major physical features . . . mountain ranges, deserts, etc.* - *Major population centers and reasons for their locations.* - *Patterns of migrations streams in U.S. history.* - *How migrations streams affect the spread of cultural traits.* - *The affect of an environmental change on a population.* - *The process of urbanization and how it affects the physical environment.* - How climatic events affect human activity. - How clearing vegetation affects the physical environment of a place.	affects citizens of both the United States and other countries. Explain that people's incomes, in part, reflect choices they have made: *education, training, self-development, and careers.* Explain different ways that people invest and save: *banks, credit unions, stocks, bonds, investments, interest, credit and loans.* **Content:** - Supply and demand - Urbanization - Invention & industry - Globalization/ interdependence - Self-development **Field Trip:** Mill in Salem **Culminating Demonstrations:** - Formal essays (2) - SRC mini-assessments - Oral presentations (2)

(Continued)

Figure 4.4 (Continued)

Student Performance Expectations	Unit 1: Civics and Government Dates: Sept. 5 to Dec. 1	Unit 2: Reconstruction and Westward Migration Dates: Dec. to Mar. 15	Unit 3: Industrialization and Globalization Dates: Mar. 19 to Jun. 14
	Field Trip(s): Salem, Oregon—capitol building Champoeg State Park **Culminating Demonstrations:** - Formal expository paper - Formal persuasive Paper - Oral presentations (2) - SRC mini-assessment	Explain how individuals, issues, and events changed or significantly influenced the course of U.S. history post–American Revolution through 1900: - *Constitutional Convention* **Content:** - Reconstruction - Migration - Geography **Field Trip(s):** Oregon Trail Head in Oregon City **Culminating Demonstrations:** - Narrative paper (biography) - Imaginative paper (westward migration) - SRC mini-assessments - Oral presentations (2)	

Grade 8 Language Arts Yearlong Plan

Student Performance Expectations	Unit 1: Expository and Persuasive Dates: Sept. 5 to Dec. 1	Unit 2: Narrative and Imaginative Dates: Dec. 5 to Mar. 15	Unit 3: Free Mode/ Technical Writing Dates: Mar. 19 to Jun. 14
All students will communicate using reading, writing, and speaking modes.	**Concepts:** Writers know how to organize ideas to inform audience of a specific topic. Writers know how to justify and share their thoughts in a precise, factual and organized manner.	**Concepts:** Writer knows how to organize and produce creative concepts with themes and/or morals.	**Concepts:** See concepts for Units 1 and 2 **Standards:** Same as previous units, but add:

Student Performance Expectations	Unit 1: Expository and Persuasive Dates: Sept. 5 to Dec. 1	Unit 2: Narrative and Imaginative Dates: Dec. 5 to Mar. 15	Unit 3: Free Mode/ Technical Writing Dates: Mar. 19 to Jun. 14
All students will use strategies that help them increase their comprehension in all stages of reading, in both fiction and nonfiction. All students will understand and appreciate human value, diversity, and interactions, both social and environmental. All students will investigate topics of interest and importance. They will select appropriate media sources, use effective research processes, and demonstrate ethical use of resources and materials. (Copyright, citation, etc.) All students will demonstrate knowledge of spelling, grammar,	Effective literacy skills (reading, writing, and speaking) are essential elements in future choices. Effective readers know how to use strategies for comprehension, monitor thinking and self-correction, engage in collaborative activities and discussion, and analyze various forms of fiction and nonfiction texts. **Standards:** Listen to and read informational and narrative text: - Use a wide variety of texts: classic, contemporary literature, poetry, magazines, newspapers, reference materials, and online information. - Make connections to text: text-to-text, text-to-self, and text-to-world. - Use comprehension strategies: re-reading, self-correcting, summarizing, talking to peers, generating and responding to questions, making predictions, comparisons, latin roots, and visualizing. Increase vocabulary: - Learn and develop new words through: Listening, context clues, dictionaries, thesauri, roots, and analysis. Planning, evaluation and revision: - Use the writing process. - Collaborative work. - Taking formal notes - Identify audience and purpose. - Use scoring rubrics. - Communicate Ideas: - Support conclusions with quotations, opinions from experts, citations, and paraphrases.	Writers use different styles to communicate ideas and express themselves. **Standards:** Same as Units 1, but add: Learn literary devices: - Literary devices: simile, metaphor, personification, symbolism, dialect, and irony, which define a writer's style. - Point-of-view: 1st person and 3rd person, limited and omniscient, subjective and objective. - Evaluate structural elements: setting, dialogue, mood, tone, subplots, climax, and themes. Conventions: - Spelling: - Commonly misspelled/misused words: among, between, bring, take, fewer, less, much, many, their, there, they're, good, and well.	Read to perform a task: - Various texts: textbooks, directions, magazines, historical documents, editorials, news stories, periodicals, and instructions. - Follow instructions. - Read visual designs and clarify: create outlines, graphic organizers, diagrams, or summaries. - Examine content and structure: read point-of-view passages and take a side to argue. - Analyze figurative language: idioms, hyperbole, onomatopoeia, Conventions: - Punctuation: colons and semicolons: semicolons to join two independent clauses, semicolons to separate groups of words that contain commas; colons to introduce a list,

(Continued)

Figure 4.4 (Continued)

Student Performance Expectations	Unit 1: Expository and Persuasive Dates: Sept. 5 to Dec. 1	Unit 2: Narrative and Imaginative Dates: Dec. 5 to Mar. 15	Unit 3: Free Mode/ Technical Writing Dates: Mar. 19 to Jun. 14
punctuation, capitalization, and penmanship. Understand, learn, and use new vocabulary that is introduced and taught directly through informational text, literary text, and instruction across subject areas.	- Use effective transitions between ideas. - Use varied sentence types (simple and complex). Conventions: - Spelling: - Use correct spelling conventions. - Learn Latin roots to improve spelling. - Read various texts for word recognition and reinforcement. - Punctuation: - Commas: to set off interruptions, to set off dialogue, in direct address, between independent and dependent clauses, to separate adjectives, to set off appositives, and to set off introductory phrases and clauses. - Quotation marks: to set off direct quotes, for special words, and to punctuate titles. - Capitalization. - Proper nouns and sentence beginnings. Writing Modes: Persuasive: Include well-defined thesis, present detailed evidence and reasoning to support argument, differentiate between fact and opinion. Expository: Opening paragraph introduces topic, supporting details that explain topic, and summarizing conclusion. Oral Presentation Standards: - Develop a purpose. Reason for giving a speech and consider intended audience.	- Changing words ending in "y" to a plural form ending in "ies." - Changing singular words ending in "f" to plural forms ending in "ves." - Punctuation: - Apostrophes to form plurals; apostrophes in place of omitted numbers or letters; apostrophes to form singular possessives; apostrophes to form plural possessives; apostrophes to form shared possessives. - Hyphens and dashes **Writing Modes:** - Narrative: Write biographical and/or autobiographical stories. - Imaginative: Fictional narrative **ELD:** **Synonyms/ Antonyms:** *definitions and practice **Adjectives:** *too + adj. *adj.+ish or ly *noun to adj.	colons after a salutation, colons between numbers and time, colons as a formal introduction. **Student choice of writing mode.** **ELD:** Adverbs Pronouns **Culminating Demonstrations:** See formal/informal assessment chart and portfolio syllabus

Student Performance Expectations	Unit 1: Expository and Persuasive Dates: Sept. 5 to Dec. 1	Unit 2: Narrative and Imaginative Dates: Dec. 5 to Mar. 15	Unit 3: Free Mode/ Technical Writing Dates: Mar. 19 to Jun. 14
	- *Outline and organize a speech. Analyze mode and apply appropriate organization before and during a speech.* - *Use credible and relevant information to convey message.* - *Use complex language and colorful modifiers with appropriate: Rate, tone, enunciation, inflection, eye contact, and gestures.* - *Use visual designs to assist message.* Listening: - *Analyze presentations.* - *Paraphrase a speaker's purpose.* - *Ask relevant questions.* Analysis: - *Provide constructive feedback.* - *Evaluate credibility of speaker.* ELD Conjunctions: Verbs: Culminating Demonstrations: See formal/informal assessment chart and portfolio syllabus	**Nouns** **Prepositions** **Culminating Demonstrations:** See formal/informal assessment chart and portfolio syllabus	

2. Use the map in that content area to plan instruction for some time to make the connections between the map and instructional design. Make revisions in the map as you and your team discover, through its use, that the sequence of standards is not logical to students or that there are too many standards launched at one time. Work only with standards, concepts, content, and essential materials. The next processes will focus on assessments of learning.

3. Star or identify on the map those standards that are tested on state assessments. Give careful consideration to the placement of these standards so that students are proficient prior to state assessment.

4. Determine the time allocation on the map by making predictions based on how long the team thinks it will take students to develop proficiency. Avoid mapping by weekly or monthly timelines. Map by assessment timelines. The purpose of mapping by assessment timelines is to facilitate the team's development of

purposeful units of study that lead students to proficiency. The focus is not on time and covering material and content; the focus is on learning.

5. Host conversations with grade levels or teams who teach courses of study that precede your course or grade level and those that follow to remove gaps and weaknesses in the maps. Furthermore, use the opportunity to request meaningful feedback from others who have not worked on the maps.

A STORY

Valor Middle School in Woodburn, Oregon, took this concept very seriously and began a thorough analysis of their standards. Valor Middle School, like Heritage Elementary, its feeder school, is faced with multiple and complex challenges. Valor

Figure 4.5 Valor Performance Data on State Assessment

Grade 8 Reading	2004	2005	2006	2007
Valor	37%	47%	51%	55%
State of OR Avg			66%	65%
Grade 8 Mathematics	2004	2005	2006	
Valor	50%	51%	56%	72%
State of OR Avg			66%	69%
Grade 8 Science	2004	2005	2006	2007
Valor	42%	36%	47%	52%
State of OR Avg			68%	69%

Grade 7 Writing	2005	2006
Valor	30%	41%
State of OR Avg		45%

Reading	2006	2007
Valor Grade 6	68%	62%
State Grade 6	80%	74%
Valor Grade 7	58%	65%
State Grade 7	73%	74%

is approximately 70% Hispanic, whose primary language is Spanish, and 29% white. At least half of the population identified by the state as white is Russian, whose primary language is Russian. Most of the students in the school have English as a second language; consequently, they are challenged to meet the Oregon State standards. They are also 95% free and reduced lunch.

Student performance on their state standardized tests has continued to improve for all students as a result of their intense efforts in mapping the curriculum and focusing on effective strategies for second-language learners.

Although they are not matching the state averages yet, they have made continuous progress each and every year. They attribute their success to their intense focus on rigorous collaboration to implement what they are learning from each other, what they are learning from their intense focus on the curriculum, from outside consultants, from their regular monitoring of student learning, and from their own reflective practices. They value their own learning and implement innovations quickly and effectively.

They began their journey by analyzing their district's strategic plan and the state curriculum standards and determining powerful student-performance expectations. Grade level by grade level, the teams developed common curriculum maps. Because the seventh and eigth grade teams loop with their students, these maps provide the teams of teachers focused coherence on the standards as they moved from seventh to eigth grade and back, from eigth to seventh. They wanted to ensure that they did not lose sight of what students needed to learn. They also developed interdisciplinary units with social studies and language arts so that students could make the connections between these two disciplines. Every summer for seven years, these teams of teachers have met for a week to revise their work. They begin their efforts every time with a review of and revisions to their maps. Sometimes, they work on developing more meaningful units of study. Sometimes, they revise their rubric for their writing. Sometimes, they debate their effectiveness in meeting the needs of all their students. During this week, they do intensive work and have time for deep conversations about what they were learning together.

During the year, these teams use their common planning time to make minor revisions to their maps and units of study, to develop more powerful lessons that incorporate new ideas they are learning from their readings and from outside consultants, and to reflect on what they are reading and how it could enhance what they are doing.

IN SUMMARY

As the community of learners develops their own curriculum maps, they have a visual navigation tool that facilitates their staying focused and staying on course throughout the year. They grow to deeply understand their standards and what they look like when students are doing them well.

- Teams establish a commitment to mapping as one of several tools they will develop together for their learning as well as their students' learning.
- They target their essential content standards as they consider their powerful student-performance expectations and course of grade-level concepts.
- They establish a format for their map, being sure to include at least the essential information: standards, concepts, content, and time allocations.
- They mark off the map in terms of time, determined by when the team believes students should perform successfully on culminating formal assessments.

- Although they may not yet have developed their common assessments together, they begin to experiment with using the map to guide their instruction and informal assessments in the classrooms.
- They host regular conversations with each other about the value of the map and the impact it is having on their teaching and student learning. They also share the challenges they are facing, establish strategies for exploring new ways of addressing those challenges, and begin to make modifications in their work.

REFLECTIVE QUESTIONS

1. In what ways does curriculum mapping engage the team in professional learning?

2. What new big ideas are emerging for you and the team concerning the value of focusing on student-performance expectations throughout the year, targeting content standards, focusing on concepts, and using the map to design assessments and determine effective instructional strategies?

3. What is the team learning about maximizing use of time to ensure mastery or proficiency of standards and concepts?

4. What challenges is the team facing? How is the team overcoming them?

5. What celebrations are in order?

EXTENDED LEARNING OPPORTUNITIES

1. Contact other teaching teams in your school or district who are developing common maps, and explore with them what they are learning and the systems they are using to make mapping valuable and purposeful for them.

2. Ask other schools in your district or area to join in the mapping process with you. Compare your work and share the thinking of all to guarantee greater alignment and to develop more rigor and precision in the maps.

3. Ask college professors or experts in the field in your content discipline to review your work and give you feedback.

5

Assessment of Student Learning

Lorna Earl (2003) distinguishes between assessment of learning, assessment for learning, and assessment as learning. In many ways, my growth as a teacher slowly and imperfectly followed that progression. I began by seeing assessment as judging performance, then as informing teaching, and finally as informing learning. In reality, all those perspectives play a role in effective teaching.

The key is where we place the emphasis. Certainly a teacher and his or her students need to know who reaches and exceeds important learning targets—thus summative assessments, or assessment of learning, has a place in teaching. Robust learning generally requires robust teaching, and both diagnostic and formative assessments, or assessments for learning, are catalysts for better teaching. In the end, however, when assessment is seen as learning—for students as well as for teachers—it becomes most informative and generative for students and teachers alike.

Carol Ann Tomlinson, "Learning to Love Assessment"

As teams grow confident in their curriculum maps, they turn their attention to their next challenging question, how will we know that they know? Addressing this question may even be more complex than determining what is worth knowing. The national movement of using assessment results to determine the retention or promotion of students, the rating of schools based on single test data, or differentiated pay for staff whose students score high on state standardized tests do not promote communities of learners, often lead students to believe they cannot achieve in school, and build resentment and resignation in those who are most essential in achieving the national vision of every child educated and skilled.

However, if the community of learners can be clear about their own values and purpose in answering the question, how will we know that they know? they can focus their energies on designing authentic, ethical assessments *of* and *for* student learning, which is at the heart of all their work. Because knowing what students know and do not know is the linchpin of all conversations about the teaching team's effectiveness with all students, having reliable, valid assessment strategies is central to a learning community's success. Results of student assessments carry profound impact on students' attitudes about themselves as learners and the value of education. Donald Graves (2002), in *Testing Is Not Teaching*, states,

> Politicians of all stripes are obsessed with testing, especially the testing of reading. Underlying all their rhetoric is the belief that testing will improve reading ability. If scores go up, this means that children have become better readers. Unfortunately, the principle means for assessing reading ability are multiple-choice tests, where children must choose the correct answer. Multiple-choice tests examine convergent thinking. They cannot tell us if the children have read books, relate one book to another, or applied texts to their own lives. Worse, the texts children encounter on these tests are often significantly inferior to those written by professional writers. Real authors order their information to engage their reader, and their characters have real personalities. (p. 1)

Theodore Rabb (2007), professor emeritus of history at Princeton University, made similar comments in his article in *Education Week*, "Assessments and Standards: The Case of History." The difficulty arises from the huge divide between the nature of most assessments and the proficiency they are supposed to demonstrate. According to Rabb, our nation will never achieve the goal of educating all children when

> individual states set standards for history consisting of a menu of information—a sure formula for "teaching to the test." Beyond a basic core of knowledge, with a few fundamental themes that would not be difficult to identify, state standards should concentrate on historical understanding. Anything less is to deprive generations of schoolchildren of the joy and insight that, for centuries, have rewarded the study of history. (p. 36)

Rabb also stresses that scores have become so meaningless that Harvard University's Daniel Koretz (2002) calls them "an illusion of success that is really nice for everybody in the system except the kids. With most standardized tests revealing nothing significant about a student's understanding of a subject, accountability has become a chimera" (p. 28). But the intense focus on these state-standardized assessments may just mask the truly damaging strategies and tools used regularly by classroom teachers to assess student learning. Individual teacher-made or textbook-written assessment instruments that teachers use regularly to make judgments of student progress eventually determine class rank, access to more challenging curriculum programming, and entrance into colleges and universities. Furthermore, these powerful instruments are often thoughtlessly prepared, not aligned with standards and concepts to be learned, neither reliable nor valid.

A principal of an elementary school had been most excited about a new reading series adopted by the district. The staff at the school had spent a year getting acquainted with the new materials. In their second year, they turned their attention to purposefully using the assessment tools that were part of the adopted textbook materials. The staff was thrilled to know that they could actually have the students take these assessments on the computer and get individual student and class reports almost immediately. As they began to have conversations about student growth over time and reflected on these instruments, they became disturbed by the data. There were no trends. Students might show tremendous growth in one marking period, and then they would lose tremendous ground the next. The results on these instruments did not align with what the teachers observed students learning in their classrooms. Puzzled, the principal began a close analysis of the reading selections and text questions of the textbook assessments. She finally ran a readability index on all of them at every grade level. The readability levels of these selections were all over the scale, regardless of grade level.

A powerful learning community takes seriously the questions: How will we know that they know? What assessments are most aligned with the essential standards and concepts we want students to learn? What varieties of assessments do we use to judge mastery or proficiency on these standards and concepts? Are our assessments designed for easy grading and scoring, or are they designed to give us the essential information we need to meet the needs of every student?

The cultural long-standing myths and historical discourse about assessment and grading are deeply engrained in education. In this discourse, the impact on students is not the central issue—the central focus is on fairness, grading practices, the roles and responsibilities of teachers, and parent reporting. Because of these deeply embedded values of assessment, grading, and parent reporting, educators have great difficulty making significant shifts to assessments as tools for learning for themselves as well as for their students (Brookhart, 2004; Guskey & Bailey, 2001; Haldyna, 1999). What is hidden in the myths is the significance of assessments in determining a student's grade, performance level, the ranking of students in a class or in a school, and the placement of students in programs. Many students at an early age are destined to low level, unchallenging, and lusterless classroom experiences (Ritchhart, 2002; Schlechty, 1997; Schmoker, 2006). Though educators pride themselves in teaching all the nation's children and are often cynical about the comparisons of the performance of students in the United States to students in other nations, they often have very low expectations for students who early on do not catch on to the assessment game or who do not yet see the significance of the impact of those assessments to their long-term success in school.

Furthermore, the values educators place on the quality of their assessments weigh heavily on a student's future. I have been disheartened many times when trying to explain to parents why their son or daughter with a 68% in some class will not graduate from high school. It is very difficult to explain to emotional parents the significant difference between a 68% and a 70% average in the yearlong life of students, which causes them to repeat a course or not receive their diploma along with their class. In many conversations with teachers about these grades, I have found very little valid or reliable information about the students' work that truly justifies the students' not passing those courses. Teachers often share their averages of work turned in and work not turned in as justification for the final big average. Over my many years as a public school administrator, during these most challenging moments I never had a teacher share with me samples of student work or portfolios that reflected the students' lack of understanding of course concepts or demonstrations of skillful applications of standards, the assessment strategies that led that teacher to make that judgment, any differentiated strategy that they used to ensure that students had every opportunity to achieve, or any community effort to extend learning opportunities when students were not getting it. Holding strong to the beliefs that the assessments they used were honestly valid and reliable and that the grading policies and information about a student's progress is 100% perfect—that the teacher might not be off by 2%—gets in the teacher's way of viewing the designing of assessments not only as a major professional community responsibility but also as a meaningful opportunity for professional learning.

My husband experienced serious, life-threatening heart-related challenges over a four-year period. I can remember one of the most challenging conversations doctors had with me. The doctors had run several tests and were sharing the results. They had decided to perform a serious procedure they believed would assist him. I asked the very pointed question, "Are you absolutely sure this risky procedure is right for Don?" Their response was, "It is our best assessment of your husband's condition based on the instruments and procedures we have and use now. Are we absolutely sure? Absolutely not! It is our best guess!" A guess? The team could see my frustration. They explained, "When we have better assessment instrumentation, we can make better guesses, but in medicine there are no absolutes."

I immediately thought about education. Educators need to develop the most powerful assessment instruments possible to determine student progress and learning and use a variety of them over time before coming to judgments. Even then, teams must accept that their judgment is only their best guess. There are no absolutes about the efforts a young person may give when he or she becomes passionate about learning. There are not absolutes in educator's guesses about who will go to college and who will not, who will become an engineer, a doctor, an occupational therapist, or a great teacher. All of those real, powerful decisions rest with individuals, the children, as they become the persons of their own dreams and aspirations for their lives!

Marion Wright Edelman (1992), founder of the National Children's Defense Fund, is a great American citizen and a hero for children. Marion was born in the South prior to desegregation. She was surrounded by a loving family and wonderful educators who taught her the value of learning and life. She dedicated her life to the total well-being of America's most needy children. Her guiding principles focus on the well-being of the total child. I think of her work often when working with teaching teams learning to develop and use meaningful, engaging assessments. Some of the greatest measures of our success as teachers and as society are never found on any classroom or state assessment instrument. In paraphrasing Edelman (1992), the true measure of our success may really be in whether we help our children know who they are, give their best effort, set goals for themselves, take family life seriously, be honest, be confident, never give up, know that they make a difference, listen for the sounds of the genuine within themselves and others, and never stop learning!

THE MEASURES OF STUDENT LEARNING

Testing may be an effective tool for measuring student learning if designed appropriately and used with arrays of other assessment strategies. Most professions today that require their members to be licensed expect students to meet certain standards on tests. However, those tests are carefully developed over time to ensure their reliability and validity. Furthermore, they are part of an array of assessment strategies. No master plumber became one based solely on a test score; there are many hours of required practice. Doctors, occupational therapists, hair designers, and teachers must complete at least one and maybe many practicums or internships as well as pass tests. These tests have long histories of development. They are standards and concept based. The test specifications and test-preparation materials are designed to guide those taking the tests to develop their confidence in passing them. These are models for teams developing assessment strategies.

However, tests are simply insufficient. Grant Wiggins and Jay McTighe (1998) made an intriguing statement in their foreword to *Understanding by Design*:

> Now, after a decade of thoughtful experimentation with tasks, rubrics, exhibitions, and portfolios, our profession has reached a milestone. In numerous districts and schools, educators now feel comfortable developing, administering, and scoring performance tasks. And—because there is no point teaching to an ambitious standard if your assessment misses the mark—today's emphasis on standards is moving performance assessment from a trendy innovation to an accepted element of good teaching. (p. v)

That performance assessments have moved from trendy to acceptable elements of good teaching may have been true prior to the major emphasis on state standardized tests to measure student and school success, but there is little evidence of performance assessments today in schools or classrooms (Schmoker, 2006). Though educators might have been experimenting with different assessment strategies in the late 90s, the challenge and pressure from No Child Left Behind (NCLB) has certainly moved performance assessments to the background. The paradox is that many authorities on the assessment of student learning focus on performance tasks as one of the best ways of knowing what students know and do not know. The works of Tomlinson (2007/2008); Chappuis, Stiggins, Arter, and Chappuis (2005); Sternberg (2007/2008); Stiggins (1997); Stiggins, Arter, Chappuis, and Chappuis (2007); Gallagher and Ratzlaff (2007/2008); and Guskey (2007/2008) all agree on the power of performance assessments, assessment *of* and *for* learning. Many of these writers focus on assessments as strategies for both understanding student learning and developing teacher competence. Throughout their writings, they reference many other researchers and assessment experts to support their positions and ideas. Although I often visit with teachers who use state rubrics to judge student writing, I find little evidence that assessment has moved beyond testing. As a matter of fact, testing has become the predominant way of knowing. More and more districts and more and more schools are developing and using quarterly, state-like assessments to ensure that their students score high on state assessments. Testing companies are rapidly embedding tests into the culture of assessment by producing expensive test banks and designing software that will allow students to take endless numbers of tests that mirror state assessments. The literature, which would guide educators to project-based, performance tasks, debates, and portfolios of student work, seems like a silent whisper in a roar of emphasis on tests as assessments of learning.

Many authorities are focusing educators' attention on the differences in ongoing, formative, continuous assessments *for* learning and formal, summative assessments *of* learning. Earl (2003) and Stiggins (1997) both support a teaching team's efforts to design and use assessments *for* learning that give students immediate feedback. Carlson, Humphrey, and Reinhardt (2003), in their work on scientific inquiry, contend that teachers who are most effective in facilitating student learning are weaving formative assessment throughout instruction. These experts in assessment recommend student observation checklists, tickets in and out the door, videotaping, and one-on-one conferencing as strategies for intervening so that students who are developing misconceptions and errors in their thinking and work are redirected before the assessment *of* learning. These "along the way" assessments guide students to succeed on assessment *of* learning.

Just as important to the learning and the teaching team is the assessment *of* learning, or culminating performance tasks. A student studying to play golf who learns an appropriate stance for addressing a golf ball, develops a skillful swing, and reads a green finds little value in this challenging work unless the golfer actually plays the game. The final culminating demonstration of learning allows students and teaching teams to analyze the culmination of all the little learnings along the way. The team's and students' analysis of student work, the final essay, the debate, the portfolio of the student's highest-quality work or artifacts of progress toward a learning goal assists them in deeply understanding student progress. Students and teaching teams can have thoughtful conversations to determine students' strengths and weaknesses, gaps in thinking, and the determination of new goals. Furthermore, the team's analysis of trends in these products assists them in redesigning maps and assessments, rethinking instructional strategies, timing and pace of instruction, and new areas for study and exploration. Most important, using a variety of assessment strategies that engage students and teachers in conversations about what students are learning builds meaningful relationships essential to learning and informs teachers and students of what is and is not being learned.

Figure 5.1   Assessment *of* and *for* Learning

Assessments for and as learning

- Are standards and concepts designed and driven
- Occur regularly with the intention of correcting before errors and false assumptions are learned
- Are often observations and conversations with students
- Are informal and usually not graded
- Provide specific and sufficient feedback for students to self-correct
- Expect students to reflect on their work, to set more challenging goals for themselves, to celebrate their progress, and to give more effort to their learning experience
- Are noted or recorded by the teaching team to determine trends in their observations and to reflect on what they are learning while teaching

Assessments of and as learning

- Are culminating projects, writings, performance tasks, or portfolios of work
- Reflect proficiency on standards and concepts
- May or may not be done with others; often are group efforts
- Reflect real-world application on what students are learning
- Expect students to create, produce, explain, justify, and share with others
- Expect students to reflect on their own learning, celebrate their progress, and set goals for their next effort

Source: Adapted from Stiggins (1997) and Tomlinson (2008).

ASSUMPTIONS

- Professional learning communities who are most successful engage in rigorous learning through designing aligned, reliable, and valid assessment instruments. They continuously learn new ways *of* and *for* assessing student learning and work to develop powerful instruments. At the same time, the team accepts that even the results of these powerful assessments are only their best guess about a student's progress.
- The more teachers are in conversation with students, the deeper the teachers and students understand the students' progress and the goals students need to set for themselves.
- As teaching teams design and use common assessments *of* and *for* learning, they develop deeper understandings of the concepts and standards for their courses of study, begin to visualize what students are actually doing when they are proficient, and explore new and different instructional strategies.
- As they learn and study how to design aligned and meaningful assessment instruments and strategies, the team grows in their acceptance and belief that

  o assessments of student learning provide information and information only on what students know and do not know based on that assessment, taken on that day;

  o all assessments of student learning are subjective (there is no such thing as an objective assessment; assessments are valid and reliable but not objective);

  o assessments are valid when they are closely aligned with standards and concepts to be learned;

  o the development of valid and reliable assessments occurs over time as teams use them;

  o assessments are reliable when they accurately and sufficiently assess the standards and concepts to be learned;

  o assessments *for* learning, or along-the-way assessments, as well as assessments *of* learning, or culminating demonstrations, are both essential to understanding student progress;

  o all assessments are designed prior to the design of units of study and instruction so that students have access to test specification and descriptions of their culminating demonstration, the rubrics that will be used to score their work, and examples so that they know what to expect;

  o assessment strategies are most effective for understanding student progress when they are differentiated based on the needs and interests of students;

  o teams garner the least information through the testing of students; the most powerful information teams attain is through student presentations, projects, conversations with students, or any demonstration of learning;

  o assessments that expect students to create, produce, explain, justify, share, and reflect on their learning provide teaching teams with the most comprehensive information about student learning; and

  o student self-assessments and reflections with peers, parents, and teachers assist students significantly in accelerating their learning.

FOCUS QUESTIONS

- What are the most effective strategies we have used to assess students along the way? What are the most effective, reliable, and valid assessment strategies that are assessments *of* learning? What are the critical attributes of both assessments *of* and assessments *for* learning?

- What kinds of assessments *of* and *for* learning will be most intriguing to students? What kinds of assessments will be most aligned with our standards?
- What are our greatest strengths in assessing student learning? What are our greatest challenges?

A VISION

The principal of the school, the school leadership team, and the learning community analyze all assessment strategies regularly to ensure that the information about student learning assists them, students, and parents in understanding how well students are doing. All assessments *of* and many assessments *for* learning are shared between grade levels and course teams. As the instruments are used, these communities of learners engage in larger conversations about their assessment instruments and processes. They are constantly asking, Are these instruments aligned with our standards and concepts on our maps? Are they giving our students and us the information we need to know about what students are and are not learning? The learning community is regularly searching for assessment strategies that are intriguing to students, strategies that give students choice, and strategies that expect students to reflect on what they are learning. Knowing the importance of interfering early when students are developing misconceptions or doing work inaccurately, the team is constantly generating new ways of assessing along the way. They revise their assessment strategies as they learn more about assessment and as they analyze their students' work.

Figure 5.2   Comparing Traditional Approaches to Professional Development With the Professional Learning Community

Traditional Perspective	*Professional Learning Communities*
• Assessments strategies are predominately tests or essays. • Assessments are often designed by single teachers after instruction. • They may be textbook- or workbook-written assessments. • They are rarely analyzed as to their alignment to state and national standards. • They are often designed for ease of grading (such as Scantron-reliant assessments).	• The learning community gives serious consideration to the question, *How will we know that they know?* and they work as a team to produce common assessments used by all. • They sense the awesome responsibility they have to ensure that their assessment strategies are as aligned to the standards and concepts as possible. • They value and use arrays of assessments *for* learning and conversations with students about the students' learning to garner sufficient information to assist students when they are not succeeding, when they are applying skills inaccurately, or when they are missing critical concepts.
• They are mainly used to get a score for recording in a grade book.	• They learn effective strategies on how to give feedback so that students discover the breakdowns in their own thinking, practices, and learning.

Traditional Perspective	Professional Learning Communities
• They are traditionally assessments *of* learning. Though feedback may be given, it is usually after the student has received a score, which has been recorded.	• Realizing the weaknesses of all assessments in understanding student learning, they provide choice and flexibility in assessment strategies to better meet the learning styles and needs of their students.
• Rarely do teachers use an array of assessments before they make judgment about a student's grade.	• They focus their energies on assessments *for* learning so that they can interfere early in the learning process and not allow students to misunderstand major concepts or skills that would result in poor performance on assessments *of* learning.
• Assessment's primary purpose is to grade students.	
• Rarely do teachers and students have thoughtful conversations about student progress on standards and concepts. They talk about a student's standing in the class based on work turned in, grades on tests and essays, and work not turned in.	• They talk frequently as a community about the progress students are making and the validity and reliability of the instruments.
	• They learn instructional strategies from each other that are differentiated based on what they are learning about what students know.
• Grades are recorded; students and teacher move on to the next unit of study.	• If students are not performing well on an assessment instrument, they look to their work to resolve the issue. They ask themselves, is this assessment really aligned with the standards? Does it meet the learning styles and needs of our students so that they can show us what they know? Did this assessment intrigue students sufficiently for them to do their best work? Did we truly give students sufficient time to learn before we assessed?
• Little if any feedback is given to students along the way to interfere in the outcomes of their performance and learning.	
• All students take the same test or turn in the same prompted formula essay on the same day at the same time.	
• The principal is rarely aware or engaged in the development of the assessment strategies used by teachers.	• Knowing the importance of assessment of student learning, principals are strategically involved as teams develop assessment strategies. They ask how these assessments show that students know the standards and concepts. They ask how these assessments will be valued by students and parents.

CHALLENGE STRATEGIES

1. As a learning team, you are beginning to feel confident about your curriculum maps. The first step is to conduct a thorough review of the research and writings about designing worthy, valid, reliable assessment strategies. Engage in this effort with an open mind and a commitment to try new strategies that may be totally unconventional. Before beginning this ambitions journey, read Marian Wright Edelman's (1992) *The Measure of Our Success.* Read it several times throughout the journey. Her stories and concepts will nurture and ground the community.

2. Study extensively the works of Rick Stiggins (1997), Grant Wiggins and Jay McTighe (1998), and Art Costa (2008). Explore and answer these questions:

- What are effective strategies for assessing student learning?
- How do you design a test that is both reliable and valid?

- What are the most effective ways to assess students along the way (i.e., assessments *for* learning)?
- How do assessments drive instruction so that all students are highly successful on assessments of learning?
- What assessments do we have now that reflect what we are learning?
- What challenges our thinking and our current practices? What are we willing to do differently?

3. After several months of research and study, begin the complex, challenging work of developing common assessments. You might consider a comprehensive review and revision of all tests. Here is a strategy for making good tests:

- Select a marking or grading period for your focus on assessments. In analyzing the student-performance expectations, the concepts, standards, and content to be learned, determine what aspect of those elements are best measured by a test.
- Spread out on a large tablet of paper those concepts and standards that are "test eligible" and begin to carefully craft test questions that best assess these concepts and standards.
- Develop at least four, preferably seven, questions per concept or standard. Make sure you have developed sufficient items to discern whether students know well the standard or concept, or if they have merely guessed a right or wrong answer. *Have we asked sufficient numbers of questions for this standard to know whether or not students know?*
- Explore using test items from texts or other materials. These test samples can be most helpful as long as these items are aligned with the concepts and standards to be tested.
- Caution: Watch out for using test items that test content—not the concept or standards (e.g., asking students the dates of the span of the cultural revolution in China is not testing the concept that corrupt governments exert inhumane power over the lives of its citizens for political gain).
- Tests are great opportunities to give students practice in test items that mirror state or national tests. Mark them on the test as state-test-like items, and let students know that they are attacking similar test items to what they will see on their state tests. Many states publish previously used tests or test specifications on their websites so that teachers have an opportunity to use them to prepare students. Just go to any state's department of education website and search for released tests or test specifications. State test items from states other than yours may or may not be aligned. Analyze them before using them. Advanced Placement and International Baccalaureate all publish test specifications. For years, test specifications have been published for the SAT and ACT. Extensive materials have been prepared, and companies have even developed training programs that assist students in scoring high on these exams. Public schools across the country are beginning to use the specifications of state tests for the same purpose.
- Produce a test specification for all tests that are assessments *of* learning. Teachers have a great opportunity to help students learn by providing them with their own teacher-made test specifications. Use the models published by states or other organizations to help the team in producing a test

specification. Teams will discover the strengths and weaknesses of their tests through their own designs and make revisions before the test is ever used. The team may wish to design the test specifications before they ever write a test item to guide their test-item bank development.

- Be sure that students are given the test specifications when the teaching team begins to teach a unit of study so that everyone knows what will be required of them to be successful. Remember to write the test before teaching. We have many examples of such processes. Medical schools, flight schools, teacher preparation programs, and driving schools all publish test specifications with sample test items and books to assist students in doing well on these tests. Giving test specifications to students helps them see what the test will look like and have an opportunity to prepare effectively.

- Note: Always give students longer passages or more difficult test questions than those given on state tests. This strategy helps students feel very comfortable about their performance on the state test, because they were well prepared.

- Help students understand the value of state tests. Let students know that these tests help them better understand what they are learning and that they will approach many tests throughout their lives. They will take college entrance exams and certification tests. State tests provide opportunities for students to learn about national standardized testing. The idea is to assist students in finding meaning in this work of showing others what they know. Help students prepare for these tests. Let them know that students of all ages all over the country prepare for tests, such as the bar exam, medical exams, and the certification tests for every thing from teaching to cosmetology. Assure them that these tests are basic to entering a profession that requires top-quality performances.

- As a team, determine to provide choices for students on tests so that they have some control over how they show you what they know:

  o Prior to testing, allow students to write test items based on the teaching team's test specifications and submit these to the teaching team to place on the test as a form of assessment *for* learning. You will have significantly better knowledge about what students know and do not know based on the quality and kind of concepts and standards the students feature in their own test items.

  o Provide ample space on the test for students to reflect on their answers. With multiple choice or fill in the blank questions, give students space and ask them to explain why they selected the answer they did. Students' responses are often eye opening as to what the test questions are really asking.

  o Allow students to choose five out of seven test questions to answer for 100% credit on a concept or standard tested.

  o Allow students to write a test question they are prepared to answer but that the team did not ask. Remember, tests are very subjective instruments. They are written by the teaching team based on the team members' perspectives of what is important. They are designed based on the team's view of how items should be structured. We have all gone into testing situations with a deeper understanding than what we could show on the test. We were often prepared to answer many questions we were never asked.

o With the world of technology today, figure out new ways to get the information about how the students scored on the test back to them immediately. When information comes back even a day later, often students have moved on. In addition, technology provides teaching teams many opportunities to provide flexibility in testing. Maybe only five students take a test a day. Through immediate information from the computer and the computer software capacity to build a new test for every child, not every student has to take a test at the exact same time in the same location. The key idea is for students to take tests when they feel confident they are ready and for teaching teams and students to receive the information they need to understand the students' progress. Have students sign up for the day and time that they wish to take a test or turn in a paper, and then hold them accountable for their own choice.

o When tests are returned to students, insist that they evaluate their own work and determine new goals for themselves that specify how they will extend their own learning to improve in the skills in which they are weak. Have students work in pairs or in small groups to teach each other and to share their own goals for learning what is needed to be learned; do not just have them make corrections on their tests. Do one-on-one conferencing with students about their performances on tests, and have students chart their own progress from test to test so that nothing is a mystery! *"I know how I am doing and what I need to do to learn more."* Time spent conferencing with students is essential to student and staff learning. Through assisting students in self-correction, goal setting, and reflection on their own work, the teacher learns more about the students. When teachers share what they are learning through conferencing with students, they identify trends in their own work and continue their own learning journey.

o Teachers often share with me that they do not have time to help students reflect on their work and set learning goals for themselves. Conferencing with individual students is just too time consuming. These strategies, if used appropriately, as a natural part of instruction, dramatically increase the students' acquisition of the concepts and standards to be learned. Educators have all the time they need to work with students personally if they value these experiences.

4. Once all tests are thoughtfully revised, focus attention on other forms of assessments *of* learning: essays, projects, performance tasks, and portfolios of student work that reflect a culmination of learning for a unit of study. Culminating demonstrations of learning, if designed thoughtfully, are authentic opportunities for students to discover real-world applications for what they are learning. They are not overnight homework or project assignments; they are assessments embedded in instruction.

5. As a team, generate multiple ideas of how the standards and concepts are applied in the world of work. Search the Internet for WebQuests and other such applications of learning. Project Lead the Way, a national effort to make mathematics, technology and its applications in engineering, and the world of work appealing to middle school–age students, has powerful examples of project-based learning and culminating demonstrations. There are entire Web sites and organizations, such as

Buck Institute for Learning (BIE), committed to project-based learning. As a team, do a thorough review of what others across the nation are designing and using with students. Of course, access the teams on creativity.

- Begin with an analysis of standards and concepts. Which standards and concepts are best assessed through demonstrations and applications of learning? What types of culminating performances give students the best opportunity for sharing what they are learning?
- Use criteria checklists, analytical scales, or rubrics for high-quality assessments that the team develops together, or use those produced by Wiggins and McTighe (1998), to guide assessment design and judge their quality to guide revisions. (See Resource I, Critical Attributes of a Performance Task or Project.)
- Design a format for defining performance tasks based on study and research. Wiggins and McTighe (1998), Stiggins (1997), and Guskey (1997, 2000, 2007/2008) all offer formats for designing culminating demonstrations of learning.
- A format and examples for designing performance tasks and culminating demonstrations and may be found in Resources J, K, and L.
- Ensure that the demonstration expects students to create, produce, explain, justify, share, and self-reflect on their own learning.
- Use as precise language as is possible so that all students have a clear vision of what they must do well to show they know the standards and concepts to be learned.
- Design assessments *of* learning first; then begin to consider how the team will assess along the way so that students are proficient and succeed in meeting the challenges and expectations of the performance task. As a team, ask these questions: What kinds of one-on-one conferences will be essential? What types of checklists will assist the teaching team and students in meeting the standards? What types of observational checklists or anecdotal notes are essential? Which checkpoints do we need? The more immediate the feedback to students, the greater the opportunity for success. Though the processes and charts for recording may not be the same for all teaching team members—some prefer to record observations in a Palm Pilot while others prefer a clip pad—what each member of the team is looking for in the observations is the same: the skills, standards, and concepts essential to be learned by students to be successful on culminating demonstrations.

6. Develop rubrics that precisely and accurately define quality. (Since rubrics are tools teams use to grade the quality of student work, more discussion about them occurs in Chapter 8.) There are no easy ways to develop precise rubrics. Rubrics define the critical attributes and the degree of quality of an artifact, a piece of student work. The descriptors have to be sufficiently clear so that users can discern distinctions and differences in the same way. In other words, the rubrics are so clear the team can develop interrater reliability. Teams begin with the list of critical attributes identified in the assessment design. They search for categories such as organization, design, resources, ideas, and content in those attributes. They apply a four-level scale to each of the categories to design their rubric. Teams find it easier to design a

rubric by placing a model or exemplar on the table and beginning to describe it at its highest scale. Then the team contrasts the highest scale with the lowest scale to establish their rubric parameters. In designing rubrics, the team considers the quality, the scale, of the attribute: for example, if talking about time the team might develop the four-level scale: consistently, persistently, frequently, infrequently. If the team is discussing quality the scale might include the descriptors: thoughtfully, engagingly, systematically, unsystematically. Some teams start by generating adverbs that describe each of the four levels of quality on the rubric before writing descriptors. They will take one category, such as organization, and describe the highest quality (4) in adverbs (thoroughly, systematically), then a 1 (insufficiently, sporadically). Then they will write the full descriptor. This process ensures equal steps for all descriptors in all categories from a 4 to a 3 to a 2 to a 1. (See Resource M, Precision in Adverbs; Resource N, Example of an Exemplary Rubric Produced by Valor Middle School Encore Teaching Team; and Resource O, Culminating Demonstration Rubric for 1st-Grade Students at Heritage Elementary.)

7. Ask students to design the rubric. Be sure to use a model with students to guide their work as well. Come to agreement as a class about a common student-designed rubric. Share these rubrics among the learning team. Find strengths and weaknesses among all the class rubrics. Share the teaching team's findings with the students for making revisions to individual class rubrics.

8. Pilot assessment strategies: Reflect on their use.

- Through the use of these assessment strategies and instruments, are we as a team getting sufficient information to determine what students are and are not learning?
- Are we using sufficient and appropriate assessments for learning so that we get feedback to students when they need it?
- In our tests, test specifications, and designs of our culminating demonstrations, are we precise enough in our language so that students have a clear vision of what they must do to show us what they know?
- Are our rubrics sufficiently precise as to attributes and quality indicators so that students clearly know what is expected and we can give precise, reliable feedback?
- What are we learning about assessment of student learning?
- What are we learning about our students?
- What revisions do we need to make in our assessment strategies?

9. Make revisions, and begin to redesign the next period of marking assessment strategies based on what the team is learning.

10. Ask teachers from other grade levels or courses of study to review the team's assessment strategies and give feedback.

11. Ask students to give feedback to the teaching team. Ask them, What about these assessment strategies were very clear to you and made it easy for you to know what we expected and share with us what you were learning? Which strategies were interesting and intriguing? What seemed confusing? What recommendations do you have for us to shift our assessments to make them clearer, more user friendly for students, and more interesting? Then use this feedback to revise assessment strategies.

A TEACHER'S STORY

A second-year teacher, Laura, from North Marion High School, Oregon, took this concept of assessments *of* and *for* learning very seriously. She was not happy with her students' lack of interest in the United Nations. She determined that for a culminating demonstration students would host a meeting of the United Nations. The Security Council would vote on an issue currently before the United Nations. Their vote would be grounded in the current political positions of each of these nations, and the national position must be supported by thorough research of translations of original source documents or reliable, unbiased resources. She thoroughly described the task to students so that they knew the expectations. The students were grouped into teams, and the learning journey began. She set the date for the meeting and the vote. Each team had a checklist and checkpoint meetings with her to guide their work, check on their progress and sources of information, problem solve, and generally stay intrigued and engaged. Students had to research current issues facing the United Nations and in particular the votes soon to come before the Security Council. They had to select an issue that the students believed had the greatest impact on the world and an impact on them in Oregon. Once they had agreed upon a current issue before the council that they wished to learn more about, they had to research their nation's perspectives on that issue and justify the position the nation would take. The issue the students selected had to do with the health of the planet. There were many times for Laura to assess along the way. She would ask pointed questions to guide students when they seemed unclear. She observed their use of sources and redirected when resources were not original work, authentic, and/or opinions of others of the nation's perspective. She would often challenge them to look more deeply or explore more thoroughly. She, too, found herself learning more about the United Nations with her students. She also realized how much her students were learning—all of them. The Security Council members representing the United States were drafting a clear proposal that would limit the world's production of carbon dioxide into the atmosphere. The students were engaged in ways she had never observed in them before. She observed their conversations and their thinking. She was surprised by their deep understanding.

The day came for the Security Council meeting. Every team was well prepared for the discussion and debate, and everyone participated. Laura observed that students who had never contributed, students who failed to turn in work, and those failing her class were involved and meaningfully contributing. After the United States made its proposal and several nations spoke, the debate began. Everyone was justifying their positions. Finally, it was time for the vote. In the end, China vetoed the proposal. Everyone in the class was stunned. China stood its ground; the proposal would not have been in the best interest for the economy of China.

Laura led the class to debrief the experience. Students shared how much they had learned about things they had never been interested in before and about the workings of the United Nations. They also began to see their world in a different light. They realized they had difficulty viewing the world from perspectives other than the United States. This led to a great discussion about points of view and perspectives and how they have shaped the telling of history.

What Laura learned is that when assessments are authentic and meaningful work for students, all students are successful in significant learning. "I have completely changed both my processes for assessing student learning and my instructional strategies. This effort has reenergized me as a teacher."

A TEAM'S STORY

A first-grade team of teachers, also from North Marion, began to reflect on the challenges they were having with their standards and concepts related to recycling, conservation, and economics. Prior to studying the importance of these standards and concepts, they had largely dismissed them, believing they were too conceptual for first-grade students to really understand. While studying powerful assessment strategies, they determined that they would have students demonstrate these concepts at a culminating demonstration to a unit on being good stewards of our resources and understanding our economy. The demonstrations of learning would occur as teams of students would sell earth-friendly art made from recycled resources and explain what they were learning about their role in caring for the planet. Each class knew the expected outcome and took on a "job" in the school that made the concepts of the power of use reduction and conservation of resources visible. One class challenged all students to take only what they wanted to eat for lunch. Students in this class weighed the food thrown away each day. Each class was rated as to how well they were doing and given feedback by the students. The students made charts to show the progress of the first-grade students and the progress of each class. One class took on the responsibility of cleaning all the desks in the classrooms. One class sold recyclable paper cups for drinking water to all other classes. For these earth (and school) friendly jobs, students were "paid" with teacher-made money. Students were going to use the money to select pieces of earth art that they wanted that all students were to make, advertise (their message about their learning), and sell at the culminating demonstration. All classes, of course, were cleaning up the environment and discovering ways to recycle things by designing and producing their piece of artwork to be sold. Teachers were weaving a conceptual understanding of our economy and the need for conservation of resources throughout the unit. Students could visibly see the outcomes. At the culminating demonstration, students only had enough money to select two pieces of art. They had to make choices. The teachers shared the deep learning of students in their classroom with each other. Students felt a sense of purpose in their work and understood they were fulfilling a job essential to the school. They shared their eagerness to buy their art. They had to count their money and determine how much they could spend. They had to make change. In reflections with students, teachers discussed the choices students made and began to deepen students' understanding of the power of advertising. Every student participated excitedly; every student developed a deeper understanding of our economic systems and ways they could contribute through conservation of resources.

A DISTRICT'S STORY

The district teacher–administrative leadership team in Northwest Allen Schools in Fort Wayne, Indiana, is very visionary in understanding the need to sustain a community of learners over time. Even though they are a fast-growing district, they have tremendous community support, which they have garnered through their commitment to excellence for every child. Worried that the curriculum would lose its coherence as they added elementary schools, the leadership team began to focus on engaging all their elementary teachers in curriculum conversations. They deeply believed that as teachers engage in meaningful conversations about what is essential for their students to know and do well and how they would most effectively assess student progress, they would guarantee to their students, parents, and community a viable curriculum experience for all students across the district. They also fundamentally believed that it was not the district's responsibility to purchase assessments or to establish a committee to produce common curriculum guides and common assessments. The leadership team committed to working with all teachers, grade level by grade level, to develop common, districtwide curriculum maps and common, districtwide assessments for measuring student learning. By engaging everyone, all would be learning and contributing to the effort. Furthermore, all those who impact student learning would make positive contributions to the products and outcomes and own the results of the team's work.

The district leadership team began its work by sharing a vision and a process for engaging the entire faculty in curriculum conversations. The team members established a simple process. They would ask administration to study essential systems for developing common curriculum and assessment strategies. Principals would engage the teaching staff in the same kinds of discovery. They attended sessions taught by Stiggins, and they researched effective strategies for assessment design. Since there were at least thirty grade-level teachers, principals, and administrators who would be working together at a time, they hired a consultant to facilitate the grade-level teams to come to consensus around the targeted standards and to design the maps and assessment strategies they all would commit to use. Everyone committed to the challenging journey.

The entire district faculty, central office administration, and principals, grade level by grade level, worked throughout a year to come to consensus about the essential targeted standards in all content areas. With those essential targeted standards, the grade-level teams developed a common curriculum map. There were many warm debates and thoughtful conversations. Everyone was involved. Many grade levels made recommendations to other grade levels to strengthen the coherence of K–5 and to assist teams in developing proficiency at certain grade levels with certain skills or standards rather than "covering" standards at a shallow level.

Once the maps were agreed upon, the grade-level teams began to focus on essential common assessment strategies. The district chose mathematics as a place to begin. The leadership team had a strong rationale for the focus. Mathematics was the greatest area of need based on state assessment data, and mathematics standards were more easily assessed. Furthermore, teachers and administrators were engaged in a implementing a new approach to teaching language arts and using new instructional materials.

Another intriguing system was emerging: teacher leadership across the district. The district leadership team decided it was time to develop their capacity more formally. These teacher leaders would receive extended support in understanding the district's vision and developing skills in facilitating teams. They would then facilitate the development of the grade-level common assessments. They would be experts in assessments and designing assessments, would ensure alignment of assessments to the standards, and would assist teams in developing worthy, valid, and reliable tools.

This natural emergence of leadership was not without its challenges. The teacher leaders were not always clear about the purpose of their work, their role, and their relationship with the external facilitator. This team reflected the lack of clarity about the purpose of common assessments. These teacher leaders were challenged most to develop competence in designing assessment strategies. In addition, there was a small underground current of mistrust. They wondered, what was the purpose of these common assessments? Who was going to use them? How would the data be used? These questions assisted the district leadership team in being clear. The district leadership team continuously assured all grade-level teams that the purpose of common assessments was to guarantee a viable curriculum to the community and that the data from these assessments was to be used by teaching teams to ensure student mastery, to reflect on their work, and to learn as a community.

Even though there were challenges, teams fell into their work naturally. They were prepared; they had done their research, understood how to develop reliable, valid assessment strategies, and were learning how to work well together. They often grouped their grade-level teams into smaller teams to accelerate the work. They always brought the entire grade level back to share work and to ensure consensus of the whole grade level on using common team-designed assessment instruments.

Each grade level did develop statelike assessment tests to be used quarterly to determine student progress on state standards, but they were not limited to this strategy. They studied state test specifications and sample items. They used released tests from many states to ensure sufficient numbers of test items. Groups developing writing assessments, projects, and performance tasks using a common format for their assessment strategies based on their research of Stiggins (1997), Wiggins (1998), and Guskey (1997).

Because the teams had been studying the attributes of quality-assessment strategies and gathering quality assessments from their own classrooms for over six months, in about one and a half days, each grade-level team had produced assessment strategies for one-quarter marking period and was ready to pilot them with all students. They were very proud of their work and curious about what they would learn.

IN SUMMARY

Learning to assess well is a major challenge for all learning teams. This learning journey is more demanding than any other aspect of the teachers' learning work. It requires in-depth study of the researchers and experts in the field. More important, it often requires a test of will and a strong commitment by teams to fight the current trends in assessment and test designs used by most teachers. Furthermore, this work is time consuming and tedious. However, for teaching teams to have the best opportunity to know their students progress, they use arrays of meaningful, purposeful assessments, consider assessment development thoughtfully, and align them carefully to standards and concepts to be learned. These teams develop both assessments *of* and *for* learning to ensure student success. They are constantly learning, from their own work and feedback from others, how to develop more powerful assessment strategies. Recognizing the impact of the results of assessments on their students, they take their work in this area very seriously and make it central to efforts of their learning community.

Principals play a significant role in nurturing the community and holding high the expectation that teams will use powerful assessments to answer the question, what do students know and not know? Because of the difficulty of this work, these leaders are patient and persistent. They establish schoolwide systems for regular review of all assessment strategies used in the school. They may organize a school-wide assessment committee that reviews assessments, looks for gaps from unit to unit, grade level to grade level, course to course, and asks questions about alignment, validity, and interrater reliability. Principals and school leadership team members educate parents about the importance of students doing well on assessment strategies and organize systems for students to share with parents their work and what they are learning.

REFLECTIVE QUESTIONS

1. What big ideas are we learning about assessment of students?

2. What strategies for assessments are we using that are having a positive impact on students demonstrating their proficiency on standards and their understanding of the concepts we want them to learn?

3. What strategies seem "activity based" rather than standards driven and concept based? What revisions should we make in them?

4. Are we using sufficient assessment *for* learning to ensure student success on our culminating demonstrations or assessments *of* learning?

5. How are students interacting with our assessment strategies? Are they doing their best work? If so, why? If not, what can we do to develop more interest and intrigue?

6. Are the rubrics and analytical scales sufficiently precise to guide students in their work and for us to give them specific feedback?

7. What new assumptions do we have about assessment?

8. What is essential for us to learn next about assessments *of* and *for* student learning?

9. What next steps are we going to take?

EXTENDED LEARNING OPPORTUNITIES

1. Design a WebQuest together. Use a model that the team believes to be an intriguing question. Be sure to focus on the standards and concepts to be learned well.

2. Have students share their culminating demonstrations at parent nights. Use these opportunities to educate parents about the connections among standards and concepts to be learned, assessments, and grades, or just celebrate students and their learning.

3. Invite community expert guests to view the demonstrations of learning and engage with students in discussions about what they as professionals are learning and how the students' work matters in the professionals' daily life.

4. Use a strategy such as a tuning protocol to review student work and to give the team systematic feedback concerning the alignment and worthiness of the assessment instrument.

5. Conduct action research using a variety of assessments *for* and *of* learning to see which tools positively provide the best information about student progress.

6. Serve as a team to review other grade-level or course assessment strategies to learn what others are learning.

7. Concentrate on feedback. Explore questions together, such as, what kind of feedback best assists students in their learning? What are the most effective strategies for giving feedback? What kinds of feedback lead students to be honestly and deeply engaged in and reflective of the quality of their work?

6

Designing Instruction

Children construct their own knowledge and understanding. We cannot transmit ideas to passive learners. Knowledge and understanding are unique to each learner. Reflective learning is the single most important ingredient for effective learning. Effective teaching is child-centered.

—John H. Van de Walle,
Elementary School Mathematics

The human brain/mind is much like a dynamic kaleidoscope. The neurosciences are telling us that, energized by genetics, experience, and culture, students literally learn from everything. And as educators we are beginning to see that what this generation of students is learning beyond the classroom is unlike anything past generations have experienced.

—Geoffery and Renata Caine,
Making Connections

"How has the telling of history shaped history?" The students looked puzzled. The teacher kept questioning, "I am wondering what voices were silenced during World War II? I wonder who was heard and why?" Students just sat silent. The questions seemed to hold their attention, but no one spoke.

The teacher continued. She shared that over the next few weeks teams of students would explore many ways they might answer the question, How has the telling of history shaped history?

Then she turned to her computer and white board. Students saw images of Winston Churchill (1940) and heard his famous speech:

> We shall go on to the end, we shall fight in France, we shall fight on the seas and oceans, we shall fight with growing confidence and growing strength in the air, we shall defend our Island, whatever the cost may be, we shall fight on the beaches, we shall fight on the landing grounds, we shall fight in the fields and in the streets, we shall fight in the hills; we shall never surrender, and even if, which I do not for a moment believe, this Island or a large part of it were subjugated and starving, then our Empire beyond the seas, armed and guarded by the British Fleet, would carry on the struggle, until, in God's good time, the New World, with all its power and might, steps forth to the rescue and the liberation of the old.

The voice of an Asian American spoke of the tragedy of losing his home at the hand of the U.S. government during World War II and how his family struggled in an internment camp. There were several clips and speeches from different perspectives—women entering the workforce; Eleanor and Franklin Roosevelt sharing their efforts to strengthen the American people, prepare them for war, and build the economy to pull the nation out of the Great Depression. There were stories from Anne Frank's (1952) *The Diary of a Young Girl*. And of course, there were clips from *Letters from Iwo Jima* (Eastwood, Haggis, Lorenz, & Spielberg, 2006). The conflicting, heart-stirring quotes, pictures, and speeches continued—stories from survivors of the Holocaust, clips from veterans from the local area—all sharing their stories, all telling history from their perspectives.

The clips were short, and the students were spell bound by the stories. The teacher told them that they would serve as a team of journalists who would publish a video newscast on World War II. In their newscast, they would answer the question, how does the telling of history shape history? She described what she expected of them, and she shared what quality work looked like. She shared the rubric by which teams could measure their own effort and judge the quality of their work. She explained how they would be graded.

After she organized them into teams, they began their adventure. Articles, original transcripts of speeches, newspaper clippings from war times, and pictures were at stations around the room with writing paper, computers, and Internet access. Students were to begin their research by reading these transcripts and making notes. They were to generate ideas with each other about what else they wanted to explore. They were not limited to what they were provided, but they were encouraged to seek other data from resources on the Internet, to contact individuals who were veterans and who were descendants of the Holocaust who lived in their community. Everyone was intrigued and engaged.

Her teaching team had been working some time to help students explain the complexity and multiple perspectives that reflected the challenges, drama, and dynamics that led to World War II and to its resolution. They were tired of disengaged and unmotivated students. They had made a commitment to each other that this year would be different. But how? They decided to do some research on their own. They engaged in readings about World War II. They viewed movies together. They searched for original newspaper articles. They explored writing and perspectives of people from Europe to Japan and back to the United States. They decided to host their own summit on World War II from their adult perspectives. They were not only intrigued, but they sometimes had heated debates about issues that were emerging.

You know our major concept has always been that the winners shape the history of any war. Maybe what we ought to be ensuring is that our students know that the tellers of history have a fundamental impact on all subsequent generations' understandings of wars and their outcomes.

Innovative instructional ideas flourished.

This teaching team reflects the challenging and engaging opportunity that teachers have to rediscover their own passions for their course content. Teaching teams have a tremendous opportunity to extend their own learning, access resources to intrigue their students, and reconnect with their own passions, perspectives and interests in their content. Furthermore, planning instruction together is fun and energizing. This collaborative work builds the instructional muscle of all on the team. As teams plan common units and lessons together, they assist each other in clarifying the standards and concepts to be learned and discover gaps in their assessment strategies. Together, they explore new, innovative strategies, and they are more open with each other about things that are not working.

Maybe the biggest challenge all teacher teams face is that young people are wired differently than many adults who teach them. Researchers in neuroscience are discovering that students who spend time with technology actually develop different neurological pathways that shape the brain to learn in new and different patterns (Caine, Caine, McClintic, & Klimek, 2005; Huttenlockher, 2002). Many students in our country have grown up with Nintendo, computers, cell phones, and Baby Einstein. Learning for this generation is fast and engaging. They enjoy intrigue and discovery. Because of these newly wired learners, teaching teams are challenged to capture their attention, interests, and engagement.

ASSUMPTIONS

- Effective teaching is standards driven, concept based, and student centered.
- To fully engage the powerful brain of each individual, teaching teams use strategies for learning that develop a sense of intrigue in the classroom. They facilitate students in activating their schema and making connections to what they are learning. Such strategies are designed to assist students in finding meaning, to apply and value the new skills or attitudes for themselves, and to understand themselves as learners.
- Teachers who plan instruction together capitalize on the ideas, skills, understanding, and wisdom of all on the team in implementing research-based strategies that lead to greater success for all students.

DEVELOPING COMMON INSTRUCTIONAL PLANS

Teacher Collaboration and Learning

When I first began working with teachers on designing common curriculum for increasing student success, I would often say, "It really does not matter how you plan instruction as long as everyone on the team knows what the students are to know and do well." I was working hard to acknowledge that not all teachers teach the same way, and many are effective with the strategies they are using. Parker Palmer (2007) tells many stories of teachers with different teaching styles, including lectures, which captivate students. I also often heard how teachers value their own unique instructional style and do not believe that they either need to or could adopt someone else's instructional strategies.

I could not have been more wrong. Current research suggests that if teachers use specific instructional strategies, more students will achieve success. Teachers do not lose their personalities or their uniqueness when they use common instructional strategies. When they are in the practice of learning together, their creativity, energy, and ideas flourish. Furthermore, teachers who plan instruction together learn from each other. They capitalize on the ideas, experiences, skills, and wisdom of everyone on the team. As they work, they support each other. They induct new teachers and develop skills in those who are struggling. All grow continuously as teachers engage in these meaningful conversations with each other.

The Student

Furthermore, students have changed so dramatically that educators are finding new gaps in the effectiveness of strategies that have worked for many years. Many theorists and researchers are challenging educators and others to consider the impact of technology on the development of the human brain.

Even in this different world where students have new neuron pathways, there are positive deviances—classrooms where students cannot wait to get to the work, classrooms where students hang around after class, lost in the learning.

Instruction That Maximizes the Power of the Brain

There are several promising instructional strategies grounded in brain-based principles: implementing inquiry based strategies; using constructivism as an approach to instruction; differentiated instruction; using reading and writing as tools for learning across the curriculum; and encouraging self-directed, reflective learners. These practices are not all-inclusive but rather, a sampling of especially promising instructional practices.

The Powerful Brain

A beginning focus for a learning team may be maximizing the research that has resulted in brain-based principles for teaching and learning. These principles assist teaching teams in understanding how people learn. They form a basis for building instruction that capitalizes on the brain's natural power to learn. Furthermore, understanding these principles guides the learning teams to build nonthreatening social environments that nurture students to become confident, self-directed, reflective learners. Caine and Caine (1994) Caine, Caine, McClintic, and Klimek (2005), Sylwester (1995), Jensen (1998), Sprenger (1999), the National Research Council (1999, 2005), and many more have focused their research on the application of brain research to classroom experiences for students. These applications assist learning teams in designing instruction that intrigues and engages students and builds confident, competent learners. The essence of their work is that the brain is a complex, adaptive system that prefers social interaction and safety. This powerful system functions best when it makes emotional connections to what it is learning. The brain has an innate system that is intrigued by complexity and is designed for searching for patterns and making meaning. According to Caine and Caine (1994) in *Making Connections: Teaching and the Human Brain:*

> The solution . . . is to deliberately embed new taxon content in rich, lifelike, and well-orchestrated experiences that require genuine interactions. In effect, we need to give students real experiences, engaging all their systems and their innate curiosity and involving them in appropriate physical movement, social interactions, practical projects, uses of language, and creative enterprises. How do we develop the appropriate connections? We do it in the normal course of events by learning from significant experience. The new information that we acquire daily is always embedded in meaningful or important life events. Some new items are preceded unconsciously. Some are deliberately analyzed and explored. Either way, they become meaningful quickly, by virtue of their being packaged in relevant, complex, and highly socially interactive experiences. (p. 47)

How might teams design instructional plans so that students are deliberately analyzing and exploring new ideas? How do teams ensure that students are learning in a social context that is both intriguing and meaningful to them? How do teams design inquiry-based approaches to learning and collaboration strategies that encourage students to ask, more than answer, questions? How do they activate a student's natural curiosity and desire to learn? How do teaching teams encourage and develop a collaborative learning environment that is both safe and nurturing?

Relaxed Alertness

According to Caine and Caine (1994), the first challenge for teaching teams is to design an emotional climate in their classrooms that focuses on "relaxed alertness." They define *relaxed alertness* as an environment that is low threat and high challenge. "The state (of relaxed alertness) exists in a learner who feels competent and confident and is interested or intrinsically motivated" (p. 17). Teachers in these classroom communities engage students in games, humor, metaphors, stories, choice, technology, guided imagery, and collaborative projects. Through these normal interactions with others students, students begin to view themselves as learners. Students develop self efficacy, resilience, and self-regulation. All of these competencies are essential for all learners in order for them to thrive in the complex, uncertain, and volatile world in which they live (Von Glasersfeld, 1989; Wertsch, 1985; Wilson & Jan, 1993).

Collaboration and Learning

Palmer (2007), in his 10th-anniversary addition of *The Courage to Teach,* shares a remarkable story of the transformation of a team of medical school curriculum designers. The medical school faculty was beginning to have growing concern about their students. They were not finding them concerned about their patients, not developing good bedside manners, and they were not supporting or collaborating with other students. He tells the story of how professors would often find articles they had placed in the library cut out of the magazines by students who did not want other students to have access to the articles. Furthermore, they did not feel that their students had sufficient time with real patients. They believed they might be skilled in learning in the classroom from their books and studies, but were not strong in meeting the needs of real patients.

They completely redesigned their standards and their instructional practices. Students were placed in groups and were assigned a real patient from the time they first entered medical school. There was a dramatic shift in students' attitudes and learning. These students grew as a community. Students who naturally asked pertinent questions taught others how to ask questions. Students who had insights and intuitions about patient's symptoms were models for others. Of course, there were skeptics on the staff. They argued that students may have better bedside manners and be more ethical, but they were sure the students' performance on standardized tests would go down. The results were just the opposite. Not only did student behavior improve dramatically, standardized test scores also went up. A collaborative, inquiry-based instruction increases the success of all students.

Inquiry and Constructivism

As teaching teams establish low-threat, high-challenge instructional environments, they are naturally drawn to inquiry and constructivism. Many researchers of inquiry and constructivism have been touted as seminal researchers in education: John Dewey (1966), Jean Piaget (1974), Lev Vygotsky (1978), and Jerome Bruner (1986). Piaget was one of the first to state that learners construct their own meaning. Dewey proposed that through inquiry, children ground their beliefs and understandings about the world. They do so through reasoning, making inferences and generalizations, observing the world and making predictions, forming hypotheses, interpreting data, drawing conclusions, and communicating what they are learning to others. Vygotsky also emphasized the importance of challenges in student learning. Vygotsky's "zone of proximal development" states that when learners successfully complete tasks that are challenging yet within close proximity to their current level of development, they gain confidence as learners and are motivated to accept even more complex challenges. Through inquiry, exploration, and discovery, students naturally make connections, activate their own schema, and construct their own meaning. Learning teams that capitalize on the thinking of these theorists are drawn to strategies that expect students to explore their own interests, understand their own learning styles, develop powerful questions, and conduct meaningful research. They regularly use stories, metaphors, and visualization to facilitate students making connections and developing deeper understandings (Resnick, 1984; Silver, Strong, & Perini, 2000; Smilkstein, 2003; Tate, 2003).

Differentiating Instruction

Recognizing the uniqueness of each learner, learning teams explore strategies for discovering the interests and needs of students and differentiating instruction. Carol Ann Tomlinson (2007/2008) has led the way for educators to develop powerful strategies for meeting the needs of all learners. Teaching teams who value a personal relationship with their students recognize the unique talents, interests, and needs of their students. They get to know students as unique individuals. They begin to explore ways to design differentiated and intriguing instruction that is varied based on the needs of their students. Through their connections with their students, teachers realize some students need more time; others need more visual assists. Some need more conversations, and some need more work with others. They build a classroom community with learning experiences that are filled with centers, varieties of learning materials, various genres, various writers, and a variety of reading levels. Students have access to technology for writing, practice skills, exploring the world, conducting research, and communicating with others. Students work predominately in teams—just like the rest of the world of work. These needs are not just needs of elementary students but of students of all ages. Teaching teams, who pretend that students in secondary schools need to practice for college and who design long, difficult assignments in which students work predominately alone, handicap those students and limits what they are learning (Tomlinson, 2007/2008; Benjamin, 2002).

Reading and Writing Across the Curriculum

As learning teams realize the social nature of all learning, they cannot underestimate the power of language and learning. Many students come to the formal learning environment of school without the language experiences essential for success in the advanced expectations of today's kindergarten. In addition, teaching teams pre-K–12 are experiencing classrooms with larger and larger numbers of students whose first and primary language is a language other than English. According to the National Center for Educational Statistics (2004) the population of English Language Learner (ELL) students in U.S. public schools between the 1994 and 2000 school years has grown substantially. Data are drawn from the Schools and Staffing Surveys (SASS) of 1993–1994 and 1999–2000. Nationally, the number of ELL students in public schools increased from approximately two million students in 1993–1994 to three million students in 1999–2000. Regionally, over half the national total of U.S. public school ELL students in 1999–2000 were in the West region. Nationally, in 1999–2000, 62% of public school students were in schools with an ELL student population of less than 1% of the school population. However, in the West, 19% of students were in schools with ELL populations comprising at least 25% of the school population; 7% of students in the West were in schools comprising over 50% ELL students. Learning teams are challenged to learn aggressively how best to meet the needs of this rapidly changing student population. In addition, those who wish to explore effective strategies for developing language in students are also faced with conflicting studies and emotional and political battles played out as research.

Some of the basic strategies in creating readers are highlighted in Debbie Miller's (2002) book, *Reading With Meaning*. Teachers create readers by

- stimulating relevant, prior knowledge so that students prior to, during, and after reading make meaningful connections to a text (Anderson & Pearson, 1984);
- creating visual and sensory images from text (Pressley, 1976);
- drawing inferences from text to form conclusions, make critical judgments, and create unique interpretations (Hansen, 1981);
- asking questions of themselves, the authors, and the texts they are reading (Raphael, 1984);
- determining the most important ideas and themes in a text (Palincsar and Brown, 1984); and
- synthesizing what they read (Brown, Day, & Jones, 1983). (p. 8)

Kelly Gallagher (2004), in *Deeper Reading: Comprehending Challenging Texts, Grades 4–12*, challenges teachers to assist students in deeper reading comprehension and scaffold the reading when they use challenging text. She emphasizes facilitating students to effective first-draft reading, to practice effective second-draft reading, to use metaphors, and to meaningfully reflect on what they are reading.

Not only is deeper reading essential learning for all students, but writing across the curriculum develops greater conceptual understanding. Expecting students to write increases their competence and confidence as communicators and thinkers. All writers write not just to share what their thinking with others but also to become clearer about what they are thinking and to organize their thinking so they can articulate it clearly to others. Elbow (1980), Graves (1983), Calkins (1991), and in the executive committee of the National Council of Teachers of English (2004) clearly state their assumptions about the connection between writing and learning. These assumptions can assist learning teams in developing engaged and purposeful writers:

- students who are successful writers view themselves as writers and use the writing process to share who they are and what they are learning;
- classrooms are filled with student voices and their lives; they believe they are unique and have much to offer;
- students make connections between themselves as readers and writers, and published authors as readers and writers; and
- through writing, students understand more deeply what they know and what they do not know.

According to the National Commission on Writing in America's Schools and Colleges (2003) in their research report, *The Neglected "R"*:

Writing is not a frill for the few, but an essential skill for all. It is not simply a way for students to demonstrate what they know . . . but a way to help them understand what they know. At best writing is learning. Yet few high school students experience many opportunities to produce thoughtful—and thought filled—papers in a variety of genres written for a varying purpose and audiences.

The commission urges schools to place writing at the center of the curriculum, to engage students in writing often and in a variety of contexts. (p. 10)

Developing Self-Reliant, Internally Motivated Students

Another major instructional interest of the learning team is developing skill in using strategies that nurture in students their natural desires to be self-reliant, internally motivated, and reflective. As teams explore this concept, they find that many of the strategies already supported through research lead their students to grow in confidence. Powerful, effective teaching teams build a climate that is nonthreatening and that nurtures the talents and interests of students. They design instructional tasks that are sufficiently challenging for students and build a sense of intrigue and inquiry that entices students into learning. As students experience success in learning, they grow as confident, competent learners. Students who are self-reliant develop skills in establishing challenging goals for themselves and their teams and skill at persisting through the difficulties. They develop skills in working hard and giving sufficient effort. They reflect in journals, learning logs, and conversations with others about their efforts to achieve their goals. Students have input into strategies they wish to use to strengthen their learning. They have the freedom to and are encouraged to skillfully negotiate with teachers and others to shape the learning in the classroom and to shape the design of assessments *of* learning. They use technology easily to learn, to share what they are learning, and to explore their world. They engage in internships and community efforts to apply the skills they are learning to make connections to the larger community outside of school (Costa, 2008; Dalton & Boyd, 1992; Marzano, 2007; Wilson & Jan, 1993)

Developing Respectful, Empathetic, and Service-Minded Citizens

Today's classrooms are rich with opportunities for teachers to develop respect in students—respect for differences in ethnicity, race, culture, and uniqueness of thought. They inspire students to discover who they are as people and to find joy and interest in being friends with others who do not have similar backgrounds, religious beliefs, cultures, or perspectives. Furthermore, through this valuing and learning from differences, students develop empathy and compassion for others and grow as citizens in a richly diverse democracy. Teaching teams can learn ways to ensure that instructional strategies engage students in service to their community and school neighbors and build democratic classrooms (Costa, 2008).

Determining a Pathway for the Learning Community

Due to the depth and wealth of research on instruction, the learning team selects an instructional focus for their learning that is of greatest interest, need, and challenge to them. They determine a process for designing units of study and lessons together. They recognize the value of planning together and acknowledge that each of their students in each of their classrooms will bring their own uniqueness to the classroom environment and may lead to essential, individual shifts in direction. Thus, the community continues to learn not only from their research and planning but also from the thoughtful experiences in the classroom.

FOCUS QUESTIONS

- Which aspects of our instructional strategies are most aligned with research on effective instruction? What challenges do we face? What do we want to learn together that will have the greatest impact on our students' success on our standards and concepts?
- Which problems should be posed to students to develop their conceptual understanding about what they need to learn?
- How do we as teaching teams develop meaningful learning experiences to capture the interest and attention of all students?
- How do we encourage students to develop their own natural desire to ask meaningful, intriguing questions?
- How do we design instructional experiences so that we immerse students sufficiently in the practice of actively processing what they are learning so that they truly own these new attitudes, skills, behaviors, standards, and concepts?

- How do we immerse students in the practice of reading and writing as tools for learning?
- What are the best approaches for working with ELLs?
- How do we build self-reliant, confident learners who know who they are, what they are learning, and who establish meaningful goals for themselves?
- How do we develop democratic classrooms, where students respect others, show empathy, and contribute positively to their school and community?

A VISION

Teaching teams who develop common instructional plans learn to implement new ideas, to try on challenging instructional strategies, and to assure alignment of instruction to standards, concepts, and assessments *of* learning. These teams are continuously studying the latest research on learning and effective instructional practices. Grounded in research and their own practices, they make thoughtful instructional decisions together. They use their instructional design efforts as opportunities to reflect on their own practices and to challenge themselves to try new ideas, to support and encourage each other, and to build learner-centered classrooms.

Figure 6.1   Comparing Traditional Approaches to Professional Development With the Professional Learning Community

Traditional Perspective	*Professional Learning Communities*
• Teachers work independently to design instruction. • They often use strategies recommended by adopted materials or resources. • Instruction tends to be whole group and activity based. • Students are challenged to do problems or complete assignments. • Instructional units and lessons tend to be designed from the perspective of teaching rather than the perspective of the students' learning. • Instructional ideas may be shared during team meetings or in the hallways, but they are rarely intentionally designed by teams. • The focus of the design of the lesson may be on maximizing use of time, classroom management, and completing assignments. • Teachers often are frustrated by students' lack of interest and believe that some things that are essential for students to	• Teaching teams intentionally design common instructional units and lessons together to ensure mastery of or proficiency on the standards and concepts to be learned as well as to ensure students effectively demonstrate their learning on assessments *of* learning. • Teaching teams are in continuous study of the research on effective teaching and capitalizing on research-based strategies to increase student success. • In designing instruction, teams work diligently to apply brain/mind principles and to develop safe and sufficiently challenging learning culture. • The teams design instruction to assist students to apply what they are learning in ways meaningful for students. • The teaching team designs instruction to engage students in using language, both oral and written, to reflect on and discuss what they are learning. • As teachers and teams of teachers use assessments *for* learning, students are grouped and regrouped based on their unique needs, and they differentiate instruction to ensure all students are successful.

Traditional Perspective	Professional Learning Communities
learn have no immediate applications to the world in which students live. • Teachers use instructional time for students to do assignments or work that is to be graded and recorded. Little thought is given to how to move students from little or no understanding to proficiency. • Noise is the enemy of an effectively managed classroom. Consequently, students are rarely in conversation about what they are learning. They have little if any time to debate and discuss with peers and teachers the concepts and standards they are learning. • Teachers do not consider ways to differentiate instruction. They sense that because they have large classes, everyone will just have to do the same work at the same time in order for the teacher to manage the class. • Students believe their job is to complete assignments.	• Students see themselves as learners. They are self-directed. They use their work as an opportunity to share what they are learning and the goals they have set themselves. • Teaching teams build a classroom culture in which all students show respect for others in the classroom and in their school. They learn to enjoy and value the diversity around them. They are empathetic toward students in need and often lend a helping hand. While discovering more about themselves as people and as citizens, they recognize and value the contributions of others who are different from them. • Principals model democracy in their leadership in the school. Staff meetings are learning opportunities, and staff teams regularly share what they are learning about instruction. The principal often does model lessons with a team and engages in study of effective instructional practices. • Principals ensure that student work is highlighted throughout the school and in newsletters to parents.

CHALLENGE STRATEGIES

1. Conduct an extensive review of the most current research on the brain and how it learns. There are many great resources for this work, but one that I have found teaching teams enjoy and find meaningful in designing instruction is *12 Brain/Mind Learning Principles in Action* by Renate Nummela Caine, Geoffrey Caine, Carol McClintic, and Karl Klimek (2005). Another essential reading is *How People Learn* (National Research Council, 1999). There are others that might be of interest to you listed in the References.

2. Use these principles as guiding assumptions in the design of all instruction, or write your own principles to guide your instructional design. Use the assumptions at the beginning of this chapter to stimulate your thinking.

3. Select an instructional approach of greatest interest to you (developing students as readers and writers, designing strategies that facilitate students constructing their own meaning, differentiated instruction, or building self-reliant, reflective learners). Conduct extensive research in this area. Select a book or several for in-depth study. Use the resources at the end of this chapter; do a search of your own. Use ideas garnered from your study to plan your next instructional unit together.

4. Determine a common format for developing standards-driven, concept-based common units and lessons. A format many teaching teams have used successfully follows. An example is in Resource P. There are also formats suggested by Wiggins and McTighe (1998) in *Understanding by Design.*

5.   Plan a unit of study together. Begin with the curriculum map. Don't forget that the standards, concepts, and content for each unit are marked by assessment timelines. Plan the entire unit, week by week, to achieve the concepts and standards and to guide students to be successful on the assessments *of* learning. Do the week-by-week planning of the unit before working on daily lessons.

Figure 6.2   Unit Design

Unit Description:

Overview of the Unit:

Description:

Weekly Overview:

	Description	*Week I*	*Week II*	*Week III*	*Week IV*	*Week V*
Standards *Objectives* *Goals*	Taken from the map Weekly objectives, goals, skills are determined from unpacking the standards					
Essential Question(s)	Determined from the concepts May be the same for several weeks, a complete unit, a term, or a year					
Assessments for *learning*	Designed prior to instruction					
Assessments of *learning*	Designed prior to instructions					
Essential Instructional Strategies (strategies we are learning and want to incorporate)						
Mini Lessons	May be designed prior to teaching; may be a response to the learning needs of the class or a sub-group of the class based on assessments *for* learning					

	Description	Week I	Week II	Week III	Week IV	Week V
Strategies for Student Reflections	Designed to expect students to think about what they are learning and not learning and to think about their thinking					
Essential Strategies for Differentiation	Designed to scaffold learning, meet learning needs and interests, address deficits					
Essential Materials						
Essential Homework	Designed to extend classroom work or practice skills and concepts being learned during instructional time					

Figure 6.3   Daily Overview for Lesson Design

	Day I	Day II	Day III	Day IV	Day V
Goal for the Day					
Essential Questions					
Mini Lessons					
Instructional Strategies					
Assessments					
Materials					
Student Reflections					
Homework					

A STORY

In observing classrooms where the teaching team had developed intriguing brain-compatible instructional plans, students are so passionate about what they are learning that they are very articulate. I was observing a group of third-grade students in Larry's classroom. They had been participating in a powerful instructional design called Storyline. The team had designed a Storyline in which students were to answer the question, how did the westward movement impact Oregon Native Americans? The students had done extensive research on the Internet and from sources provided by the teaching team. In Storyline, students become characters and develop narrative fiction as well as nonfiction text to explain social, political, and scientific principles and phenomena in the world. Teachers design incidents along the way that cause the students to clarify their perspectives, seek additional information, or conduct research before coming to new conclusions. The students had studied the life of the Salmon People, Native Americans in Oregon. They knew how the people lived and worked. They also had researched how the Lewis and Clark expedition had brought disease and death to the people. They were furious.

The classroom conversations with these students were really quite inspirational as well as funny. I had come with a group of sixth-grade teachers, who were studying and intrigued by Storyline as a strategy for designing instruction, to visit with the students. We had decided to go visit with these third-grade students to determine the impact Storyline had on their learning. Larry, the third-grade teacher, had prepared both us and the students for the experience. The sixth-grade teachers just began asking questions of the students about what they were learning. The students began sharing their learnings and their stories. They were focused on the destruction of the Salmon People. They shared about the lives of the Salmon People—how they lived, how they dressed, what their homes were like. They shared their interviews with people in their community who were descendents of the Salmon People. They shared about the destruction that had almost wiped out the Salmon People when the Lewis and Clark expedition brought diseases and technology. As they talked, they moved from their chairs toward the sixth-grade teachers. They became more and more unaware of where they were in the room and more and more aware of what they wanted their visitors to know. I was humored by their passion and humbled by the clarity of their thinking.

Later, Larry shared with us that, toward the middle of the Storyline, he realized that students were developing only one perspective, that of the Salmon People. His students were intensely empathetic toward the impact of the westward movement on the Native Americans. He had to discuss this issue with his team who had designed the Storyline. The team agreed that they had actually designed the lessons to ensure empathy. They decided to make some shifts in their work so that the children would also understand and value the courageous challenges and the positive impact of the Lewis and Clark Expedition on the expansion of the United States, which was actually one of their state standards. Those third-grade students would not accept the shift. They had been immersed in the concepts that westward movement had wiped out the Native Americans and their way of life forever. They had made up their minds! All members of the teaching team agreed that the next unit would focus on the values of exploration, discovery, and inventions that bring about powerful, positive changes in the world.

No one was more impressed with the learning of those children than the sixth-grade teachers. Off they went to their own learning team to implement some of the strategies that they could apply to their work with sixth-grade students.

IN SUMMARY

Communities of learners make the most effective instructional decisions when they work systematically and effectively to use research-based, brain-based strategies in their classrooms. As they study and work together, they challenge themselves to meet the unique needs of today's learner. They lead and facilitate students to construct their own meanings, to explore their world, to be powerful users of language, and to see themselves as readers and writers. Teaching teams seek ways to differentiate instruction to meet the unique needs and interests of their students and to capitalize on the power of technology for enabling students to explore their world. They work diligently to ensure a safe and nurturing learning environment that challenges students to be self-reliant, confident, and competent and to build democratic classrooms where respect, responsibility, empathy, and laughter are norms.

REFLECTION QUESTIONS

1. What new ideas about instruction are emerging for you and for your team?

2. Which ideas are intriguing enough for the team to explore in depth? How does the team want to explore them?

3. How do you best want to plan instruction together? What format will be best for the team to use?

4. How often will the team reflect on their instructional plans? How often do team members want to support each other using new strategies so that they can give feedback and learn from the models teachers are for each other?

EXTENDED LEARNING OPPORTUNITIES

1. Use the Tuning Protocol, from Easton's (2008) *Powerful Designs for Professional Learning,* to determine the effectiveness of a challenging instructional strategy and its impact in increasing student learning.

2. Design model units of study and lessons as exemplars. Develop a rubric for a quality unit and lessons to guide the development of future units of study.

3. Observe other teachers in your building or in other schools or districts implementing strategies of interest to your team. Host a conversation with these teachers about their struggles and successes in using the strategies effectively.

4. Analyze a WebQuest or inquiry-based project as to the instructional approaches that seem most effective in achieving the objectives of the unit.

5. Videotape each other implementing the new approaches to teaching, and use the tapes to highlight effective, precise implementation and areas for growth.

6. Use videotapes from Video Journal or other organizations that produce tapes of high quality lessons.

7

Analyzing Student Work and Monitoring Student Learning to Inform Instruction

Teachers are able to think more deeply about their teaching and what students are learning. As they see what students produce in response to their assignments, they can see the successes as well as the situations where there are gaps. In exploring those gaps, they can improve their practice in order to reach all students.

—Joan Richardson, NSDC

The process of studying student work is a meaningful and challenging way to be data-driven, to reflect critically on our instructional practices, and to identify the research we might study to help us think more deeply and carefully about the challenges our students provide us. Rich, complex work samples show us how students are thinking, the fullness of their factual knowledge, the connections they are making. Talking about them together in an accountable way helps us to learn how to adjust instruction to meet the needs of our students.

—Kate Nolan, Director of Re-Thinking
Accountability for the Annenberg Institute of School Reform

Professional conversations are enriched when they are focused and structured, when all participants consciously use the tools of inquiry, data generation, and nonjudgmental behaviors, and when each member of a professional community takes an active role in the conversations.

Through dialogue, we learn from processing our experiences and we enlarge our frame of reference beyond the episodic events of every day school life. We know that holding conversations about work is essential to professional growth and development, because reflecting with others on experiences amplified our insights and complex learnings.

—Thomasina D. Piercy, *Compelling Conversations*

If we individually make the effort to ensure that each child is known in our system, our organization will be a caring learning community that knows and lifts each child.

—Les Ometani, Community School Superintendent,
West Des Moines, Iowa

Through the processes of designing curriculum maps, common assessments, and common units and lessons, teams accelerate their learning and the learning of their students. With a coherent common curriculum, assessment, and instructional plan, they are ready to shift their attention to analyzing their students' work and to monitoring student progress as strategies for accelerating their own learning and the learning of each student.

ASSUMPTIONS

- As the professional learning community systematically monitors student progress on standards and examines student work, they reflect on their own work through the work of students.
- The learning team determines essential shifts in their curriculum, assessment strategies, and instructional plans as they host meaningful conversations and analyze data.

Conversations Around
Student Work to Inform Instruction

I have been amazed at the number of books written about the power of conversations, such as *Crucial Conversations* (Patterson, Grenny, McMillan, & Switzler, 2002), *Fierce Conversations* (Scott, 2002), *Compelling Conversations* (Piercy, 2006), and *Turning to One Another* (Wheatley, 2002). According to most of these authors, conversations open teams up to new ways of observing the world. Some of the most compelling conversations are those held by teachers as they examine student work and monitor student progress. Teaching teams who have been developing common curriculum maps, common assessment strategies, and common instructional plans have been hosting powerful conversations that have led them to meaningful work. Through these continuous, structured conversations, they are guaranteeing a viable, common curriculum for all students. They learn together as they design assessments, units of study, and lessons. They have a sense of fidelity about their curriculum. Just as important, they develop trusting relationships that facilitate team members having open and honest conversations to share ideas and seek help. They have a foundation for hosting purposeful, meaningful conversations about student learning to truly inform their instruction.

Focusing on the Progress of Each and Every Student

One of the great challenges is for teaching teams to personally know and serve each and every individual in their schools. Kids count! However, the numbers of students served by single teachers and students' schedules make individual relationships between teachers and students almost impossible. These powerful relationships are essential for students and teachers to know each other, value the learning that is possible, and know what students are and are not learning. A quote from Parker Palmer (2007) in his book *The Courage to Teach* reflects a perspective sometimes held by teaching teams on students simply because students and teachers have not developed a trusting relationship that allows for genuine engagement in and intrigue around a subject.

> The way we diagnose our students' condition will determine the kind of remedy we offer. But we teachers spend little time thinking with each other about the conditions of our students, about the maladies for which our teaching is supposed to be the cure. We have nothing to compare with the 'grand rounds' common in hospitals, where doctors, nurses, therapists, and other professionals collaborate in diagnosing a patient's need. Instead, we allow our "treatments mode" to be shaped by the thoughtless stereotype of students that float freely in faculty culture.
>
> The dominate diagnosis, to put it bluntly, is that our "patients" are brain-dead. Small wonder, then, that the dominant treatment is to drip data bits into our students' veins, wheeling their comatose forms from one information source to the next until the prescribed course of treatment is complete, hoping they will absorb enough intellectual nutrients to maintain their vital signs until they have graduated.
>
> Our assumptions that students are brain-dead lead to pedagogies that deaden their brains. (p. 42)

Regardless of the challenges, teaching teams have a better opportunity to know their students well when they work together (Blankstein, 2004; DuFour, Eaker, Karhanek, & DuFour, 2004; Hord & Sommers, 2008; Piercy, 2006). They create systems for gathering data on student learning one standard at a time, one student at a time. They meet in small groups and with individual students to continuously confer about student learning. The slope of a school's achievement is fundamentally dependent on the slope of each individual student's learning (Piercy, 2006). The community of learners takes each student's progress seriously. They share ideas with each other. They notice students who are not achieving. They host structured conversation with school counselors, other teams in the school, and their principal to share what they are observing in their data, to share what they are doing, and to seek additional support or ideas. They have a "whatever it takes" attitude.

Gathering data student by student, standard by standard, and concept by concept can seem overwhelming for a team. Thank goodness for technology and Excel spreadsheets. Piercy (2006), in her book *Compelling Conversations,* shares many tools that are very useful to teams in beginning the task of understanding student learning one student and one skill at a time. Teams work diligently to design data-recording processes that are easily used by everyone on the team and that record a student's progress, standard, and concept by standard and concept.

Figure 7.1   Format for Recording Student Data

Student	Standard A		Concept 1		Standard B	Concept 2
Student A	Assessment/Date *Writing sample/9/12*	Score *3*	Assessment/Date	Score		
Student B						
Student C						

Some teams may choose to keep individual portfolios on all students that result in a summary chart such as that in Figure 7.1.

Another essential facet of understanding student learning is to examine actual student work. The Aspen Workshop on High Schools recommended in its summary report for the Transforming High Schools Task Force that the continuous and collaborative examination of student work is a critical strategy for transforming high schools. Not only will analyzing student work transform high schools, it will transform any learning team by engaging it in authentic study and reflection on the work of students in contrast to examining the work of teachers. A teaching team's eagerness to collaboratively analyze student work and to use the findings to shift their own work profoundly impacts student success.

Using Protocols

Several organizations and experts in the field of assessment have developed essential protocols for examining student work. Through thoughtful, precise use of these protocols, teams have a process that guides them to new and innovative ideas. Protocols structure analysis to courageously analyze trends in student performance on standards, to determine the impact of the intense efforts or implementation of a new innovation on student products, to determine breakdowns in the teaching team's work, and to generate new instructional ideas.

Professional learning communities use a variety of protocols for examining student work. As Lois Easton discusses in an interview with Joan Richardson (2001):

Of course, teachers have always "examined student work." But traditionally they've done it solo.

It's been a solitary experience rather than being a collaborative experience. Their learning is limited because they've been working alone. . . .

...ional learning community, we can't be shy. We ...: (paras. 2–4)

...on:

...ers work together to study student work is one ...ssional development strategies in recent years. ...lps teachers intimately understand how state ...their teaching practice and to student work. ...more deeply about their teaching and what ...see what students produce in response to their ...successes as well as the situations where there ...gaps, they can improve their practice in order to reach all students. (para. 5)

Paraphrasing Easton, Richardson explains:

> Intensive examination of student work is key to creating and sustaining a professional learning community, Easton said. She also sees it as a crucial element in deeply understanding the connections between what teachers think they're teaching and what students are learning.
>
> When schools talk about being data-driven, people think of test scores, graduation rates, absenteeism rates. I don't know that those numbers are really very meaningful. Student work is a powerful example of student data. It's much more meaningful to go to real student work—a math portfolio, a sculpture, a videotape, a piece of writing—than to look at numbers about that work. (paras. 6–7)

However, Richardson writes, "Examining student work is more complex than simply pulling together a group of teachers to chat about a student's paper or project" (para. 8).

But it is important to realize that looking at student work is risk free, and everyone learns.

Many organizations have designed a variety of protocols to provide facilitated structure to team conversations, Collaborative Assessment Conference developed by Harvard's Project Zero, the Action Reflection Process developed by the Education Development Center, and Standards in Practice developed by The Education Trust. All protocols are designed to connect analysis of student work with teacher teams' work. Teams examine student work to determine the strengths and weaknesses in what students are learning and to make recommended shifts in the team's efforts. The learning community is challenged to end conversations with a carefully crafted plan of action to ensure that all members have a common vision of the new innovations they are going to implement.

An Example

A protocol for analyzing student work that I developed and have used with teams follows the scientific inquiry process. The community has been working with students on developing competence on a set of standards and concepts, as designed on the team's curriculum map and through their common unit of study. The students are engaged in a common final assessment that results in a project, product, debate, or piece of writing—a product that can be examined by the teaching team.

1. Before any student work is graded, the team determines that they wish to examine all the students' work to better understand the progress their students are making in meeting the standards and understanding the concepts.

2. They seek a facilitator, a fellow teacher in the school trained in facilitating protocols for analyzing student work, and they host an organizing meeting.

3. The facilitator establishes the timeline, outcome, and agenda for the first session. The teachers discuss how their instructional efforts have been working in their classrooms and their successes and challenges. They share what they have been learning about their students' progress through their ongoing assessments *for* learning.

4. The team spends significant time determining a strong open-ended, genuine research question to guide their analysis. They ask, are students becoming more proficient users of precise, descriptive vocabulary since our last assessment of their learning? In what ways are students organizing their ideas and using logic, reasoning, and reliable sources in their persuasive speeches for their debates? The team members continuously ask themselves, what do we really want to learn from examining student work?

5. Once the team is satisfied with its research question, the facilitator turns to the question of how the team will conduct the study. Will the team choose random samples of student work? Will the team consider only each teacher's best three samples? The team debates the best process for answering the research question or questions. The team also considers whether or not they have interrater reliability or if they need to test their reliability before they start their research.

6. Once the process for gathering data is determined, the facilitator assists the team in establishing a timeline for completion of individual work.

7. Before the initial session is closed, the facilitator turns the team members' attention to determining how they will record their data to insure they all follow the same process.

8. The facilitator suggests the team generates a hypothesis as to what they believe they will find through their research.

> I really think we will find that students are very persuasive, but may not be using deductive and inductive reasoning. I also think they are having difficulty distinguishing reliable, credible sources to make their points. I think we are going to see far more descriptive and precise vocabulary this time.

9. The team begins its research as planned. If the documents to be examined are long or if teams must view videotapes, the research may take extended time. The facilitator guides the team in setting the second meeting date to give team members reasonable time to conduct their individual analysis.

10. Once the team members have analyzed their students' work and gathered their data according to the agreed-upon process, the facilitator guides the team to generate comments about both the strengths and the weaknesses that they discovered through their critical analysis. The facilitator plays an important role in ensuring that the team focuses and answers their research questions.

> I certainly found in my research that more and more students (75% of those that I examined) were using descriptive words in their writing, but sometimes I felt that the students just took them out of the thesaurus or

off our classroom word walls. Students did not seem to make their choices based on the message they wished to share.

Well, I saw excellent use of precise and purposeful vocabulary in about 60% of the work I examined. My data includes appropriate use of such words as. . .

The facilitator captures the team's findings in terms of strengths and weaknesses on white boards, paper, or a computer and projection screen so all can see.

Figure 7.2   Example of Data Findings

Finding	Examples
Seventy percent of the student work I examined used very precise vocabulary and figurative language appropriately. The majority of these students used vocabulary we have been working hard on to ensure they have oral and written fluency.	Paper A: *diligently, explicitly, "as cold as the frozen river," putrid, tepid . . .*

11. Once everyone is confident that the strengths and weaknesses in student work are stated clearly, the facilitator turns the group to the conversation about possible remedies. The facilitator asks, what do we think are contributing factors that we control? What do we need to celebrate together? What are possible remedies to our challenges? What new ideas might we explore as new solutions? What do we need to learn together?

Figure 7.3   Format for Data Analysis Conversations

Findings	
Strengths?	Weaknesses?
Celebrations?	Challenges?
Remedies?	Learnings?

12. Finally, confident that the team has generated promising ideas for both immediate application and for exploration for future learning by the team, the facilitator guides the team to develop a plan of action.

Figure 7.4   Plan of Action

Results:

Rationale:

Steps	Persons Responsible	Resources Needed	Timeline	Evaluation

Teams may examine student work across several assessments to identify trends in student performances. They may explore work from several different grade levels or courses of study to determine growth. The team's primary questions may be, are more students being more successful on certain standards because of our intense effort to impact that learning? What different strategies are students using to solve their mathematics problems now? How well are they explaining their work now? Are students becoming more proficient at organizing their thinking? Are they meeting the expected proficiency standards on the state rubric? The key is that the microscope is on student work.

As they regularly examine their students' work, the team members become naturals at generating new and creative ways to assess student learning, differentiate instruction, scaffold learning along the way, and to intervene when students are not being successful. They become creative in grouping and regrouping students based on their unique skills as teachers and on student needs.

Pyramids of Interventions—Pyramids of Extensions

As teams host meaningful conversations generated from their ongoing collection of data of student work, teams develop pyramids of interventions and extensions for students not achieving and for those accelerated in their learning. Through developing pyramids, the learning community generates ideas for implementing innovative instructional strategies to best meet the interests and learning needs of students. They also consider strategies to extend learning opportunities for students not demonstrating proficiency on the standard. The book *Whatever It Takes* (DuFour et al., 2004) emphasizes the need for teams to consider the strategies they may use to extend and intervene in student learning. The pyramid is built as teams consider which interventions the team members can do in their own classrooms, what they can do together, what needs to be done with other teams in or across the school, how they can do intensive work with students outside of school hours, and which interventions actually work when school is not in session. The national effort to intervene with students with special needs and identified under federal legislation as needing special education services in school through Response to Intervention is the strategy that can be extended to all students. The professional learning community should be committed to doing whatever it takes to ensure the success of all students. The most effective and the least costly are classroom interventions. Students know their classroom teachers, and teachers can maximize the student–teacher relationship to make natural the intervention process. As teams use strategies from the pyramid that are not interventions that can be done in the classroom or on the team, the interventions become more costly in terms of time and resources, as well as less effective. However, the team is committing to do whatever it takes to succeed with every student.

An Example of a Pyramid of Intervention

The purpose: The learning team is committed to doing whatever it takes to ensure the success of each student. Students who are not finding success in school develop greater and greater feelings that they are not successful at "doing school." They lose self-confidence and do not put out their best effort. The pyramid of intervention gives the teaching team ideas for interfering prior to a student's loss of self-confidence or before the student fails to understand significant, essential standards and concepts necessary for success.

Each level of the intervention that moves away from the classroom is less effective and more expensive. The most effective and least costly in terms of time, organization, and money is Level I intervention.

Level I: Interventions most effective in the classroom

Level II: Interventions most effective across the team

Level III: Interventions most effective across the school

Level IV: Interventions most effective outside of school

Level I: Interventions Most Effective in the Classroom

Critical Attributes of Level I Interventions

- Students' needs are met in the regular classroom.
- Teachers differentiate assessments, instruction, time, and/or grouping of students to catch students up.

Examples

- Teachers have daily one-on-one conferences with students who are in need of assistance.
- Students not developing understanding are given more time to understand concepts and complete work than other students.
- Students are given more models and examples through mini lessons.
- Teachers allow students to show them they know in different ways: Some students produce plays, some write them; some tell a story, others put on a debate.
- Teachers pair students struggling with students accelerating to host a conversation about what is to be learned.
- Students give each other feedback on their writing using a common rubric.
- Students are given a contract or goal-setting process to focus their work on what they need to learn.
- Students monitor their own progress.

Level II: Interventions Across Teams

Critical Attributes of Level II Interventions

- Teachers share the responsibility of the achievement of all students on the team.
- They establish regular time in the instructional day for the team to support and tutor students who are not being successful.
- They match teacher team strengths with student needs.
- They do not establish rewards and punishment systems; they work to increase the success of students by expecting students to give more effort to their learning and having the confidence that they will.
- They celebrate little successes in learning so that students are inspired to try harder and produce greater quality work.

Examples

- The team establishes a system for tutoring students who are not meeting the standards.
  - At the end of each three- or six-week period or a marking period following the completion *of* assessments of learning, teams analyze student performance data to determine who is not achieving on which standards.
  - The team determines the needs of students and groups them by those needs. All students' needs are addressed.
  - The team places each student in an intensive tutoring session for one hour during the school day with the teacher who has the greatest expertise in the area in which the student is struggling.

(Continued)

(Continued)

- o Teachers use differentiated instructional strategies; teaching occurs—not just completion of workbook assignments or homework.
- Teaching teams regroup their students for unique lessons once a week.
- Teachers on the team weekly mentor a group of students not in their classrooms to keep them on tract and be their advocate.

Level III: Interventions Most Effective Across Schools

Critical Attributes of Level III Interventions

- All teachers in the school and the leadership team accept the responsibility for students who are not succeeding.
- The leadership team in the school establishes a system for schoolwide support for students not being successful.

Examples

- The leadership team establishes a schoolwide system for intensive instruction.
  - o The school leadership team regularly gathers data from all learning teams in the school and analyzes student-performance data.
  - o They assign every person in the school to a group of students for tutoring during the school day. They may also invite regular parent or community volunteers to assist in the tutoring process.
  - o This may occur daily or weekly depending on the analysis of student needs.
  - o Assessment strategies are used regularly to determine progress. Student groups stay together until they develop proficiency in the skills essential for them to learn.
- A schoolwide counseling and mentoring program is established to meet the social and emotional needs of students.
- Organizations, such as local businesses and Kids Hope USA, are invited into the school to mentor students.
- Students share what they are learning and their work with younger students.

Level IV: Interventions Most Effective Outside of School

Critical Attributes of Level IV Interventions

- All teachers in the school and the leadership team accept the responsibility for students not succeeding.
- The leadership team in the school establishes a system of schoolwide support for students not being successful that occurs after school hours.

Examples

- The leadership team establishes an after-school tutoring club.
- Students are mentored by business leaders in the community who have similar interests.
- Students engage in ropes courses to inspire them to challenge themselves.
- Students take regular trips to local museums or businesses to see real-world applications of what they are learning.

The learning community must also consider a pyramid of extension for students who are accelerating in school. For too long, students who are learning rapidly are bored in school. These pyramids expect students to work deeper on issues they are learning or find meaningful partnerships beyond school for application.

Example: A Pyramid of Extensions of Learning

Purpose: Many learners of all ages often have the competencies expected in a standards-based curriculum. Because of their skill levels, they sometimes lose motivation for learning. Recent researchers on high school students suggest that students will produce higher-quality work if they are expected to do so. Furthermore, just accelerating students horizontally through the curriculum may not best meet the learning needs of students. A more effective strategy may be to differentiate learning and assessment experiences for students to take them more deeply into understanding the concepts and competencies on their grade level, while also taking into consideration their unique needs and expanding their skills essential for living successfully, empathetically, and joyfully in our complex world.

As teacher teams work together, they create new strategies to extend student learning and to continuously engage all in meaningful work.

The purpose of the pyramid is for teaching teams to design strategies that grow in complexity and that challenge students at their instructional level.

Level IV: Self-directed learning, service oriented

Level III: Community-focused, project-based learning

Level II: Performance-based learning

Level I: Natural extensions of current classroom standards and instruction

Level IV: Self-Directed Learning, Service Oriented

Critical Attributes of Extensions of Learning at Level IV

- Students engage in self-reflection concerning their passions and interests and seek opportunities to explore them.
- They discover that they have a profound impact on the future of their community, state, nation, or world.
- They set challenging goals for themselves and a plan of action to design and put into place a program or process that heightens awareness of major issues and suggests possible solutions.
- They engage others in their vision, establish a system for monitoring their own progress, and share what they are learning and accomplishing publicly.

High School and Middle School Exemplars

- Students work side by side with a person in the community who conducts research or studies particular aspects of the community, such as medical, scientific, or technological research, economic trends, political research, or social issues. The student becomes a part of the team and conducts extensive research with that person. The team of community member and student establishes a goal, determines a plan of action, determines quality indicators for the work, and monitors progress. The student and community member produce a research paper publicly sharing their findings.
- Students explore the needs of children who are homeless in their community. They design a system for addressing the health care and educational needs of these students through extensive research; they develop a position paper and present it to the city council for consideration.
- Students conduct extensive research into the health care of children in the United States, gather data, make comparisons to other nations, and draw conclusions from their study. They determine an effective strategy for improving the health of children in the United States, write an editorial to send to their local newspaper or news magazine, and share their findings with their U.S. senators and state representatives.
- Students conduct extensive research into different strategies for conserving fuel in the United States and establish a position paper to be shared with local U.S. senators and legislators.
- Students conduct extensive research into water pollution in the area, gather data to determine trends, research the impact of efforts to prevent water pollution, and make recommendations about solving important issues.

(Continued)

(Continued)

- Students design WebQuests for younger students to learn about important community, social, and ecological issues.

Elementary Exemplars

- Students conduct extensive research about the local government's executive, judicial, and legislative branches, interview key figures in the government, and establish strategies for students' voices to be heard, concerning the safety and security of children.
- Students establish a community legal system in their school. They set up a court, elect a judge, determine punishment for students not following rules in the school, and pass judgments. They monitor their effectiveness and report their findings to the school administrators and school board.
- Students conduct extensive research on the attitudes and positions of candidates for local offices and take positions based on what the students believe is in the best interest of children.
- Students interview immigrants in the area, write nonfiction narrative poetry that reflects the stories and lives of those who came to the area, and publish the poems in a book of poetry to be kept in the library and shared with other children. They share with others what they learned about immigration and the journeys and lives of those who live in their community.
- Students interview centenarians and share their stories, the challenges they face, the needs they have from society, and the attitudes, health habits, and relationships that have helped them live long lives. The students draft their findings and propose a strategy for the continued health and well-being of individuals approaching 100 years of age.

Level III: Community-Focused, Project-Based Learning

Critical Attributes of Extensions of Learning at Level III

- Students work in teams to engage in community efforts and/or project-based learning strategies of interest to them.
- They set team goals and establish a plan of action to design and put into place a program or process that brings awareness of major issues and their possible solutions to the community.
- They engage others in their vision; they establish a system for monitoring their own progress and for sharing what they are learning and accomplishing publicly.

All Grade Levels

- Students, working with local parks and recreation leaders in the community, design an outdoor learning center for students in the district and community. They conduct research and gather data concerning the environment in the community, determine a place for the center, establish a design, and seek district and community support.
- Students working with the local environmental agencies develop a community organic garden. They conduct their research and determine the essential characteristics of an organic garden. They establish a design plan for implementation, a process for funding the project, and a presentation to city council about the plan to seek approval and begin work. They monitor their progress until the garden is functioning and used by the community.
- Students evaluate and judge laws being recommended to be passed at the local, state, and national levels; they conduct research around those issue, establish positions, and host a meeting with or write a letters, to support their positions, to a congressperson.
- Students produce digital photography or artwork of the impact of natural disasters or historical events such as war or economic conditions on the lives of the people, tell the stories of people impacted in narrative text, and share those stories and photos on the Web.
- Students interview war heroes, share their stories with others, and host an evening celebration for people in the community to support these individuals.
- Students investigate careers in which math has real-world applications, and they post information about those careers on the school Web page regularly to interest students in mathematics.

- Students host a United Nations meeting on an authentic issue before the National Security Council. They conduct research, take an authentic position as one of the five nations on the Security Council, and share what they learned about the value of the United Nations in national security.

Level II: Performance-Based learning

Critical Attributes of Extensions of Learning at Level II

- Students produce writings and products that are models or exemplars for other students.
- Their work reflects real-world applications for their learning.
- They reflect on their progress in developing 21st Century skills.

High School and Middle School Exemplars

- Students research the causes of the American Revolution and host the First and Second Continental Congress for other students to observe. They use authentic artifacts, share quotes for the historical figures who shaped the future of the country. They share all the issues that were essential for the Continental Congress to address. They share the impact that the American Revolution, the Bill of Rights, and the Constitution have on our lives today.
- Students explore different writers and the impact they had on shaping thinking during their time in history. In an essay and in public sharing, they explain the impact that these authors continue to have today and in particular on them.
- They design technology-driven systems for sharing the application of mathematical concepts in the world.
- Students engage in a WebQuest. They reflect on what they are learning and share their exploration and discoveries with others.

Elementary Exemplars

- Students develop a "treasure chest" or "travel trunk" that reflects the journeys of their ancestors to the new world. They share songs, poetry, cultural artifacts, maps, and challenges of their ancestors.
- Students adopt a group of younger students to teach them about the value of reading and math in the real world.
- Students connect through the Internet with a school in Japan or China or another country and share cultural and life experiences through writing to each other.
- Students monitor their own learning and set goals for themselves. They develop a journal and a portfolio to share their progress with others.
- Students design and establish a butterfly garden in their school, write about the continuous changes in the garden, and reflect on what they are learning.

Level I: Natural Extensions of Current Classroom Standards and Instruction

Critical Attributes of Extensions of Learning at Level I

- Students engage in a more complex experience of a current assignment and share about the experience with the entire class.

All Grade Levels

- Students develop a PowerPoint presentation explaining a major concept students are learning.
- Students conduct research on a topic students are learning to discover current, real-world applications of that topic.
- Students accept responsibility for teaching a key component of what students are to know.
- Students read authentic documents in their original version and compare abridged versions to what they are reading.

(Continued)

(Continued)

- Students design puzzles and problems for others to solve that reflect the learning.
- Students create graphic representations of the concepts and competencies to be learned to facilitate their own and other's learning.
- Students produce a DVD of an aspect of what they are learning to share with others.
- Students retell a reading from different perspectives: different perspectives from history, different retellings of myths from different characters' perspective, and so on.
- Students design a chart, map, and timeline to reflect westward movement. They develop a diary of experiences using Lewis and Clark's diary as a model.
- Students research the history of their community and produce a "history book" to reflect the founders, the industries, the trends in population, the changes over time, and the accurate timeline, including significant events.
- Students research, design, and produce scaled models of engineering masterpieces and share what they are learning about math and engineering.

FOCUS QUESTIONS

- What standards, skills, and concepts are essential for us to monitor student by student? What are our most powerful standards?
- What data-gathering tools are essential for us to monitor student progress? What assessments *of* learning and assessments *for* learning will we use to gather our data?
- What systems do we need that will facilitate us hosting meaningful, focused conversations about individual student's progress?
- What questions do we authentically have that we would like to answer through examining student work? What protocols best meet our needs?
- What strengths are we discovering in our analysis? What challenges are persisting? What new challenges have appeared?
- What modifications do we need to make in our curriculum map, our unit design, and our assessment strategies *of* and *for* learning?
- What do we need to do to support students who are not learning what we want them to learn? What strategies are essential for students who are accelerating?
- What do we now know we need to learn to increase our effectiveness with all students?

A VISION

In order to strengthen their practice, learning teams regularly monitor student progress and examine student work. The learning community uses specific data-gathering tools and protocols for the practice, based on the intended purpose for the study. They deeply believe that student learning and the work they produce is a result of their curriculum-mapping efforts, their assessment designs, and their instructional plans. They examine student work with authentic research questions and structured protocols. They systematically make judgments about student learning and student work and determine a course of action to celebrate what students and teachers are learning and accomplishing together. They develop effective skills and strategies for redesigning their work when they discover gaps in their students' thinking and achievement. When faced with persistent problems, they engage in research and discovery to ensure their continued pursuit to increase their effectiveness.

Figure 7.5 Comparing Traditional Approaches to Professional Development With the Professional Learning Community

Traditional Perspective	Professional Learning Community
• Teachers grade student work and record their scores in their grade books. • Teaching teams rarely examine their own students' work to reflect on the impact they are having and to change their practices. • Teachers rarely examine student work to determine their own professional learning needs. • Principals monitor state data and share the data with staff. The expectation is that teachers will identify the needs of students based on these annual tests and design instruction to meet their needs. They often reshape the school plan based on the data.	• Teaching teams determine a systematic process for gathering data on student learning one standard at a time, one student at a time. • Teaching teams consistently use the data on student learning and their examination of student work to determine the strengths and needs of students, to group and regroup students, and to extend learning opportunities and time for students in need of assistance. • Teaching teams reexamine their own work based on their analysis. They make modifications to strengthen student learning. They revise the new unit about to be taught to close gaps in student learning. They revise units they have just completed to ensure they are ready for the next year. They reflect on the quality of their assessments in learning what they needed to learn about students and revise these tools as well. • They design strategies for extending learning opportunities for students within the school day. They may regroup students in their own classrooms to provide intensive work on gaps in student learning. They may also regroup students among all the teachers, capitalizing on the strengths of the teaching teams and matching those strengths to student needs. • They celebrate student success and learning as well as their own success in teaching, and they energize the community to learn new strategies. • If persistent issues are evident in student work, the learning team initiates new study and research to discover new ways of reaching all students. • Principals are intensely focused on student learning. The principal hosts regular conversations with each team about student learning. The principal problem solves with teaching teams about strategies for meeting the needs of each student. The principal and the teaching team develop schoolwide and extended day tutoring, teaching, and support systems for students who are not showing progress through classroom and team interventions and extensions.

CHALLENGE STRATEGIES

1. Establish a system for monitoring student learning standard by standard. Think big and start small. Monitor standards and concepts that students seem to have the greatest difficulty learning, or monitor one or two standards that have the greatest impact on all other standards, such as inferential reading of nonfiction text

or persuasive writing. If you choose to monitor too many standards, the team will become discouraged with the process and feel it is overwhelming. Chose a beginning carefully! Design a simple system. Excel spreadsheets are easy to use. There are computer programs that are beneficial, but be cautious. Some programs are extremely expensive and require extensive teacher effort, taking away time for professional learning.

2. Establish a schedule for hosting regular conversations about student progress using the data. Analyze data across classes and host meaningful discussions about the possible causes of high levels of achievement, inadequate progress and possible remedies, and celebrations that are in order.

3. As a team, establish a timeline for regularly analyzing student work. Determine the protocols that best meet the needs of the team. The team will find a variety of other protocols for collaborative analysis of student and teacher work in the document produced by the Center for Collaborative Education (2001).

4. In establishing the research data-gathering process, be sure to consider and test for interrater reliability. If team members are scoring products differently, the data will not be valuable in making judgments about student learning.

5. Gather data from this work to regularly analyze trends in student learning. At least four times a year, reflect as a team on the strengths of students in their performance on standards, the challenges, the possible causal factors from the team's work that lead to students' strengths and weaknesses, and possible steps that the team needs to take to modify its work as well as extend learning opportunities for students.

6. Design systems for extending learning time for students based on their needs. Regroup students within the classroom to ensure each student's needs are met. Share the responsibility of student learning among the team members. Match groups of students with teachers on the team who have expertise in the students' greatest area of need. These intervention sessions may occur daily, weekly, or biweekly depending on the team's assessments of students' needs.

7. Design a pyramid of interventions and a pyramid of extensions to intervene when students are not being successful or to extend learning opportunities when students need to accelerate or deepen their learning. Add to it regularly as the team learns.

STORIES

Monitoring Student Learning

At Hart Elementary in Austin, Texas, the principal leads an effort to monitor every individual student's performance in reading and mathematics every three weeks. She wanted to be sure that every student would be successful on the state assessment at the end of the year. Working with teaching teams, she hosted regular conversations with teams about the progress of their students. Each team shared evidence of student work and performance on assessments of each student. The team regularly explored strategies for differentiating instruction in their classrooms. Through these discussions, the principal discovered that a new teacher was really struggling. Students in this classroom were actually losing ground. She went to a master teacher in the building who was willing to teach two classes at the same time and model for this new teacher how to teach for mastery. He observed in the classroom for several weeks. He then began coteaching. He eventually developed the skills and competence he needed to increase the success of his students.

In addition, students were grouped by their deficient skills for tutoring during the day. Everyone in the school had a group of students. Tutoring for all began at a common time before lunch. The principal, all support staff, and all teachers had a group they were responsible for teaching. Each tutor knew exactly what skills each student needed and worked diligently to ensure the deficits were remedied. Students stayed in these groups for three weeks. As assessments were given again, teams met again, and students were regrouped based on the new findings. Some teachers had more students than others. Some accepted the challenge of working with students that had much to learn. Tutors were matched to groups based on their expertise. Because of this intense effort, students who often would not be successful performed very successfully on their state assessments.

Working With One Student at a Time

I was working with a group of administrators, community leaders, and teachers in the Franklin Township Community Schools, Indianapolis, Indiana, in facilitating their strategic plan. However, during a passionate discussion about the importance of all children learning, a high school teacher spoke earnestly about an effort at Franklin Central High School to ensure all seniors graduate. She admitted quite frankly that the idea was almost generated too late to have a major impact, but the school leadership team had identified all high school seniors who were at risk of failing at least one course, which would prevent them from graduating. High school teachers volunteered to see each one of these students through to graduation and to do whatever they could to facilitate the learning, to inspire the student to meet the standards expected, and to graduate. This teacher had volunteered and was working with two students. She had intervened in time, and both students were going to pass their courses. She had worked with their teachers about what was preventing them from passing. She met with the students at least weekly to teach, facilitate completion of work, encourage attendance, and inspire them to want to earn the credits needed to graduate. At the end of one of her sessions with one of the students, the student grew quiet and simply said, "Why do you care?" She was taken aback by the question at first. Then she began an elaborate explanation of the importance of his graduation to his life. She shared that she genuinely cared about him and wanted the best for him. He replied, "You're the first! I wish you had begun working with me when I was a freshman."

The effort of this small team of teachers in this high school was so successful that the next year they did begin working with students much earlier to ensure their graduation. Their focus on winning one student at a time led to a new slope in the graduation rates for that high school.

Examining Student Work

Each time I facilitate a protocol to examine student work with school teams, I am reminded of the power of teacher collaboration and conversation. I had requested two leadership teams from two different schools to model a tuning protocol strategy during a district's staff-development session. A tuning protocol is a system for assisting teachers to "tune" their practice based on the examination of student work and the lessons that produced it (Easton, 2008). One team had brought some ungraded student writing samples. The students had had a common prompt and the team had been working hard to ensure students were developing sentence fluency and using accurate conventions of the language. In engaging in the tuning protocol, this team presented their student work to another team. The first team had spent some time establishing their research question and was ready to participate in the protocol. I made sure that the listening team clearly understood the research questions and the instructional processes followed by the presenting team. After the listening team examined the student work presented to them, they began to give cool and warm feedback. They began to explore strategies about how they might address the challenges presented in the questions. They focused on the students' work as though it were the work of their own students. Everyone began generating multiple ideas. Both teams became very involved. The team that had brought the student work was intensely listening and taking notes. Both teams forgot they were modeling for others. In debriefing the session, everyone who participated believed they had new ideas to use in their classrooms. Furthermore, the team that received the warm feedback shared, "The warm feedback felt really good. We are often so critical of our work and our students' work that to hear how good the work is was really nice!"

Within a forty-minute conversation, teachers were energized and eager to try new strategies that they had generated. Maybe just as important, they celebrated the efforts of teachers to lead students to produce quality work. Everyone who participated had a renewed passion for teaching and learning.

IN SUMMARY

Teaching teams deepen their understanding of their students' learning through an intense focus on monitoring student progress one student at a time and through examining student work. Using structured systems for gathering data and structured protocols for examining student work facilitates the processes and allows the conversations to generate new ideas and plans of action for revising teacher work. In addition, as teachers generate new ideas, they develop skill in designing and using pyramids of extensions and interventions so that all are learning.

REFLECTIVE QUESTIONS

1. How will the team monitor student progress standard by standard, student by student?

2. How will the team examine student work in structured and meaningful ways to inform instruction?

3. How will we use what we are learning to intervene when students are not learning and to extend learning when students are accelerating?

EXTENDED LEARNING OPPORTUNITIES

1. Implement action research to try on new strategies to achieve the standards and concepts.

2. Inquire as to how other teams in schools around the country are monitoring student learning and examining student work. Request them to engage in a conversation with you about their interventions and extension strategies. Establish a blog to keep the conversation going.

8

Using Effective Grading and Parent Reporting Practices

Assigning grades and reporting on student learning is an inherently subjective process. It is an exercise in professional judgment that involves one person making evaluative decisions about the achievement or performance of another person. For this reason, efforts to develop completely objective grading or reporting systems are largely in vain.

Valid grading is not a mechanical process. It's also not a process that can be made more valid with mathematical precision or through the use of sophisticated technology. Teachers at all levels must be clear about their grading standards, the various components that will be considered in determining grades, the criteria that will be used to evaluate those components. Buy while clearly articulated standard and grading criteria can enhance the validity of grades as accurate reflections of students' achievement and performance, the process of grading still involves thoughtful, reasonable, but imperfect human judgment and should be recognized as such.

—Thomas Guskey and Jane Bailey, *Developing Grading and Reporting Systems for Student Learning*

No matter who we are or what we are doing in life personally or professionally, we are continuously asking ourselves, How are we doing? How do we measure up? Students and parents have an intense interest in how students are doing in school. Early on in a student's school life, students begin to measure themselves and their success by others. The nation's grading systems, class-ranking systems, and parent reporting systems all seem to reflect a national value of judging one student's work in comparison to another. I wonder how learning would be valued if it were measured against a standard?

As the learning community clarifies and designs its assessment systems, the natural question is, How will teachers let students and parents know how well students are learning in school? Because the community of learners has been engaged in authentic, honest efforts to design curricula and assessment strategies, designing grading systems may seem easy. However, the challenge in redesigning grading systems that reflect mastery of the curriculum standards seems to be counter to the cultural and historical discourse on grading (Brookhart, 2004; Guskey, 2000; Haladyna, 1999). If the learning community is ready to challenge itself to design a standards-driven grading system, the community will carefully consider when and what to grade, how to engage students in the process, and how to assist parents in understanding their students' progress. The team will be challenged by outdated but pervasive, valued practices of class ranks, grades and their impact on student participation in extracurricular activities, seat time versus proficiency, extra credit, extra efforts, and many other current practices that determine a student's grade.

ASSUMPTIONS

- As learning communities develop standards-driven and concept-based grading systems that reflect proficiency and mastery, they begin to question current practices and search for more effective ways of communicating student learning and progress.
- Translating learning into numbers and grades is often ineffective and always an imperfect process.
- The more precise the tools used by learning teams to determine the quality of a student's work and assign grades, the more reflective those grades are of the learning.
- As teams give students specific and timely feedback and delay grading, they motivate students to continue working and put forth more effort.
- The more students are engaged in assessing their own work, the greater the learning.

REVIEW OF LITERATURE

The Latin word for *assessment* means to "sit beside." As teams learn strategies for assessments *for* learning and give students immediate feedback as they sit beside, they often become uncomfortable with current grading systems. They begin asking, What is to be graded? How will it be graded? By whom? What will the grade mean? If some students have extra help and more time to revise their work, is giving them the same grade as another student who did not need as much support fair? As teaching teams spend time together to establish a grading system that reflects mastery of the curriculum standards and concepts, they may begin to realize the gap between what the team wants the grading system to reflect and what current practices really are (Guskey & Bailey, 2001; Marzano, 2000). As they question their practice, the learning community begins to generate new ideas for moving closer to grading that reflects learning. They consider not taking grades too early in the learning process. They begin to make judgments about the quality of their assignments and the importance of those assignments for their understanding of student learning (Bloom, 1976). They stop giving extra credit for work that does not reflect progress toward achieving the standards—extra points for attending activities at school—losses of points for work turned in late or for lack of sufficient headings.

They become skilled at developing clear criteria for grading. The team uses these criteria to design highly rigorous rubrics and analytical scales (Guskey & Bailey, 2001; Marzano, 2000). They use models or anchors of student work to ensure their fairness in assigning grades. To make sure they are scoring student work the same among all their students, the team regularly tests itself to ensure interrater reliability. They share these rubrics with students so that students may increase their success. They use the rubrics to give students specific feedback along the way.

Furthermore, learning teams extend the opportunity for students to see their growth over time by developing skills in using portfolios of student work. Over time, students collect samples. The team develops critical skills in leading students to be assessors of their own work so that they are in continual revision and know how to do better. The team may establish a system for students to submit their portfolios to a jury or panel of judges that may include experts in the field as well as their teachers and peers (Resnick & Resnick, 1992).

Most important, the learning community values and realizes the importance of students' self-evaluation and goal setting in producing high-quality work. They know and capitalize on the fact that when students understand clearly the criteria for success, they are more motivated and increase their productivity. As students engage in establishing the criteria for success and in peer- and self-evaluation, they become a community. Though the notion of class rank keeps students considering the competitive nature of school, they often realize that by helping others learn, they, too, are strengthening their skills and deepening their understandings (Biggs, 1999; Brown, Rust, & Gibbs, 1994; Costa & Kallick, 2000). As students develop a sense of ownership of their own learning, they set goals for themselves and measure their progress. They develop the essential lifelong skills of becoming more reflective and of valuing the power of giving more effort to work.

In addition, the learning community begins to consider the weight or importance of some kinds of work over others. Some assessments are weighted more than others. In addition, the team wants to ensure that the grades truly reflect learning. Giving grades too early and averaging those grades with grades after students have learned establishes a grade that is not an authentic reflection of what the students know and understand. Finally, the team carefully designs new and more effective strategies for communicating student progress and learnings with both students and parents.

FOCUS QUESTIONS

- How do we ensure that the grades students earn reflect mastery of the standards and deep understanding of the concepts?
- How do we establish a grading process or system that reflects growth in students?

- What tools are essential for us to develop to bring precision to the process of determining grades?
- How do we engage students in evaluating their own work and determining their own grades?
- How do we separate effort and work-ethic grades from proficiency grades on standards to honor both?
- How do we ensure that parents are regularly and adequately engaged in conversations with their students and their teaching teams to understand what the expectations are for student success and how well their students are doing in school?

A VISION

Teaching teams use analytical scales and rubrics to judge the quality of student work. Students and teachers have a clear understanding of how these tools relate to the grade and the grade's relationship to mastery of the curriculum standards and concepts. Teaching team members ensure that the tools they use to grade student work are precise and used effectively to assist students in their learning. They often seek assistance from experts in the field to ensure they are measuring the right things. These experts may also be used to jury student work. The learning team works together to ensure that they are applying the tools appropriately themselves through testing their interrater reliability. They engage students in the process of assessing their own work and the work of their peers. Teaching teams guide students to assess their own work, set goals for themselves, and develop systems for using portfolios to reflect on what they are learning and to monitor their progress.

Figure 8.1   Comparing Traditional Approaches to Professional Development With the Professional Learning Community

Traditional Perspectives	*Professional Learning Communities*
• Teachers develop individual grading systems for their own classrooms.	• Teaching teams develop systematic grading systems that reflect mastery of or proficiency on standards and concepts.
• Grading occurs regularly. Teachers often hold the perspective that if they do not grade student work, students will not do it.	• They ensure that students and parents understand how students will be graded.
• Grades are often given early in the instructional term, prior to students having sufficient opportunity to develop proficiency in standards or deep understanding of concepts.	• Teams develop precise tools for measuring quality work and use anchor work or models to assist students in understanding what quality work looks like.
• Grades often reflect completion of assignments rather than proficiency or mastery of the curriculum standards and concepts.	• Teacher teams develop skills in giving immediate and specific feedback. They postpone grading to motivate students to continue giving more effort to their work. They assist students in developing portfolios of their work and in using rubrics and analytical scales to monitor their progress.

Traditional Perspectives	Professional Learning Communities
• Even though some grades are weighted and count more heavily—daily grades may not count as much as test grades—all grades are recorded and count. • Extra points may be given for activities not related to mastery of or proficiency on standards—turning in notebooks, attending concerts. • Points may be taken away if work is not turned in on time, regardless of its quality. • Grades are viewed by the teacher as objective and essential for motivating students to turn in work. • The principal may be aware of each teacher's grading system and may have conversations with teachers who have large numbers of students who are not passing their courses.	• They learn effective strategies for engaging students in self- and peer-feedback and grading, goal setting, and reflecting on their progress. • They recognize the difficulty and imperfectness of translating student learning to a number, and they work diligently to ensure those numbers are as reflective of learning as possible. • These teams host regular parent conferences and parent nights for demonstrations of student learning so that parents can see the growth in their students. • As a team, they develop skills in training students to lead conferences with their parents so that students articulate effectively their learnings and use their portfolios and artifacts as models. • Principals communicate regularly with teams about their grading systems and engage in the work of ensuring that the grading systems are as closely reflective of proficiency on standards as possible. They use multiple systems, student handbooks, parent newsletters, and parent conferences to communicate the grading systems and the meaning of these grades to student success.

CHALLENGE STRATEGIES

1. Host a team meeting and explore the assumptions held by the team about grading student work.

- Consider carefully those assumptions that motivate students to produce high-quality work and those that do not.
- Discuss thoughtfully the assumptions that undergird the practice of grading student work and students' willingness to complete work that is not graded.
- Chart which assumptions held by the group are assisting students in producing quality work and becoming self-reflecting and those assumptions that are getting in the way.

2. Conduct book studies of *Transforming Classroom Grading* by Robert Marzano (2000) and *Developing Grading and Reporting Systems for Student Learning* by Thomas Guskey and Jane Bailey (2001).

3. Use these guiding questions to reflect on what the team is learning: What big ideas are emerging through our readings? What models or examples did we discover in our reading? What implications are there for us in our development of a purposeful and thoughtful grading system?

4. Identify what the team would envision the common grading system to be like if the purpose was to ensure that grades reflect student mastery or proficiency

on the standards and deep understanding of the concepts. Generate this vision on chart paper so everyone can see the concepts and ideas and debate about them. Identify the critical attributes together.

5. Determine what the teams' strengths and weaknesses are in light of the new vision. Through this analysis, design a system for grading the next unit of study.

6. Review all rubrics used by the team to ensure they are rigorous and precise. Ensure that these precise rubrics are not content specific, but standards driven and concepts based. So that, when used throughout the year, students begin to improve their work because they become very familiar with the scoring rubric. If state-assessment measures have a common rubric for their scoring of writing, speaking, or math work samples, use the state's rubric. They are often well thought out and aligned with standards. Beware of online rubrics. Though they may help generate new ideas, they often do not align with the team's state standards and often do not use precise language.

7. Determine how the rubric will be used during the formative assessments or assessments *for* learning. Teams might not use the entire rubric during the first assessment of learning. When teams are working on organizational skills, they may guide students to consider only the attributes related to organizational skills. As the year progresses, more components of the rubric may be used until the entire rubric is used for assessment and grading.

8. Some teams may choose to use an analytical scale for assessments for learning. These scales are not as precise as rubrics, but they are helpful tools in assisting students and teaching teams to identify the critical attributes of a piece of work and to determine missing elements.

9. As a team, develop strategies for giving specific feedback using the rubric or analytical scale to motivate students. Design instructional strategies that expect students to use the rubric to evaluate their own work and to give others specific feedback. When students are too general in their self-evaluation or when giving peer feedback, guide them to your work as a model for their work. Teach them to give specific feedback and to be precise in their evaluation of their own work. Let them know the importance of specific, precise feedback in increasing the quality of their work and their grade.

As a team, establish a goal-setting and portfolio system so that students authentically reflect on what they are learning, set meaningful, strategic learning goals for themselves, and develop strategies, such as portfolios, artifacts, or collections of their work, that reflect progress.

10. Establish a system for parent reporting that reflects mastery of standards and understanding of concepts. Be sure to develop strategies for assisting parents in understanding the reporting system and the importance of student mastery in the long-term success of their children.

11. Explore and develop systems for hosting parent nights and student-led conferencing. Both are opportunities for parents to visit with students in the presence of other students, parents, and teachers to share and celebrate the learning that is occurring in the classroom.

TWO STORIES

I had the privilege of attending a parent-literacy night for first-grade students at Heritage Elementary. I had been engaged with the school learning teams from some time, but I had never been present at one of their many planned parent nights. It was a great opportunity for me to observe the joy of first-grade students reading to their parents and siblings and to see student work that was a result of the assessment strategies we had all designed together. Joy, enthusiasm, laughter, tears, and authentic sharing of student writing and reading filled the cafeteria. As I have shared before, Heritage has three predominant languages: Russian, Spanish, and English. I could hear all three languages as I moved among hundreds of students, their parents, and teachers. I regularly sat down with these students and their parents and was amazed at the reading and writing skills of first-grade students. I was also enthralled with the teaching going on. Often, parents were learning new vocabulary in a language new to them. One little girl caught my attention. I had to sit down at the table as an observer. However, she would not allow me to be an observer. She was reading to her parents in Spanish. Her book was written in Spanish, but she was translating for me—telling me what the word was in Spanish and asking me to say it and then translating that word to English so I would know what it meant. Only for a while did I keep the tears back. All of a sudden, right in front of me was a six-year-old teacher. She was confident in her own learning, eager to share, and unwilling to allow me to not know what she had written.

The second story is even more personal. My second daughter challenged the educational system regularly. She was a gifted musician and found little enthusiasm for other courses. I had many conferences with teachers throughout my years of working to diligently and persistently ensure her success in school. As we entered middle school, I had grown accustomed to starting the year off with a parent–teacher conference. Although I worked in the district as an administrator, I would begin each conference with, "I know you know I am an administrator in this district, but I am coming to you today as a parent. I love my daughter very much, and I need your help; I want you to know. . . ." By the senior year, the calls and conferences were routine business. At the end of the junior year, my daughter had decided to sign up for AP English IV. I did every thing I could to discourage her: "You do want to graduate from high school, don't you? This course will be demanding; you cannot just skip assignments or set your own dates for turning in work, you know!" She was insistent. She had heard great things about the teacher, and she was going to take the course!

I was prepared. I was going to parent night, and after the large group session with the teacher, I would ask for my conference meeting. When I walked into the classroom, I was intrigued by the high-quality samples of student work all around the room. Mrs. Palnac started off the session with how excited she was about her new classes and each one of her students. She shared how important their success was to her personally and how committed she was to each and every one of them. She had my attention. She shared the expectations for the course, the rubric for measuring their success, and the quality of the writing in the room. My heart sank. Then she said, "There is no one who cannot do this quality work." She shared her grading system. She then commented that some times students struggled at first, but that was a natural part of learning to meet rigorous standards. She said some grades, especially early on, may not be as high as we have experienced in the past, but she guaranteed that if we all worked together, all students would score high in her class and on the AP exam. As the session ended, I started my original approach. Mrs. Palnac stopped me; she said, "Let's give Erin a chance!" I have never seen Erin so motivated. She did struggle at first with the complexity of the reading and the high-level expectations of the writing, but something was different. From time to time, she even engaged me in reflecting with her on her work and her progress. Something was really different! As Mrs. Palnac promised, grades were lower at first, but Erin always knew how to improve. She had many conferences with her teacher and her peers; she kept revising her work. She received so much feedback on such a regular basis that she did not have an opportunity to slip between the cracks and not turn in work. Erin was learning what it meant to put out more effort, and she did score high in her class and on her AP exam. So did all of the students, as promised. More important, Erin is an excellent writer today and uses writing skills regularly in her career as an occupational therapist. When the year was over, I was overjoyed and was preparing my thank you note to this wonderful teacher when I received a special gift in the school mail. Mrs. Palnac had written the first note. She told me how much she enjoyed Erin as a student, what a thoughtful student she was, and how hard she worked in her class. She knew Erin had a bright future, and she was thrilled she had had the opportunity to be a part of her life! I still have the note.

Not only had this teacher kept her promise and inspired Erin to do her best work, but she also gave one tired parent hope.

IN SUMMARY

Teaching teams who use grades effectively to reflect students' proficiency or mastery of standards and deep understanding of concepts postpone grading to motivate students to continue to give effort in their work. Furthermore, they do not want to give students grades too early in the learning process. They develop a common process for grading for all students on their team or in their courses, and they ground those policies in sound assumptions about the relationship between grading and student learning. Grades are based on the use of precise tools, such as scoring guides, analytical scales, and rubrics, so that students know how to improve. The professional learning community is continually working to ensure rigorous, precise rubrics. They ensure the quality of the use of these tools by regularly assessing their interrater reliability. Students are very clear about the expectations for scoring high and are actively engaged in the process of understanding and producing quality work. Students often share what they are learning on parent nights and during student-led conferences. And as always, based upon what they are learning through their own observations of student-led conferences, parent nights, peer assessments, and one-on-one conferences with students, the professional learning community is redesigning its curriculum maps, unit designs, assessments, instructional plans, interventions and extensions, and grading systems to increase student success.

REFLECTIVE QUESTIONS

1. Which big ideas from the teams' readings, research, and questioning of current assumption about grading are of greatest interest to the team?

2. What celebrations are in order?

3. What new grading practices and systems need to be designed and implemented?

4. What next steps will the team take to ensure that grading reflects student mastery of standards and concepts?

5. What new strategies will the team use to ensure students and parents understand student progress?

EXTENDED LEARNING OPPORTUNITIES

- Host focus groups with students and parents on the importance of grades to them, and solicit their ideas about what matters to them in grading student work.
- Practice expecting students to write narratives explaining what they are learning, their progress, and their goals to their parents as attachments to formal grading systems.
- Annually retune rubrics based on what you are learning through using them to score student work.
- Annually, as a team, use the rubrics on student work not scored to determine your interrater reliability. Discuss the differences in your scores to increase common thinking and reliability.

9

Leading Schools to Sustain the Effort and Fulfill the Promise

Leaders matter. What leaders say, do and think—and who they are when they come to work each day—profoundly affects organizational performance, the satisfaction they and those with whom they interact derive from their work, and their ability to sustain engagement with their work over the period of time necessary to oversee significant improvement.

—Dennis Sparks, *Leading for Results*

The growth and development of people is the highest calling of leadership.

—Harvey Firestone, Founder, Firestone Tire and Rubber

Students and staff thrive when leaders, regardless of where they are within a school system, focus on student learning, commit to their own professional learning and the learning of others, build strong relationships, shape a collaborative culture, muster resources, and hold a vision for success. The new model of a school leader is one who continuously learns.

—Hirsh and Killion, *The Leading Educator*

received an e-mail that saddened me greatly. Yet, it happens all too often. The person who e-mailed me was one of the members of the leadership team, in one of the stories I shared, that had had great success in raising student performance. He told me that all the work that had been done to build a professional learning community had been lost. The three key leaders in the central office had moved on. The principal had been reassigned; two people on the leadership team, one an assistant principal in the school and another teacher leader, also aspiring to be a principal, were not selected as the principal. One of these two went on to become an assistant principal in another district. Other members of the leadership team had become disillusioned and had recessed to their classrooms. Teachers had moved away from collaboration back to isolation, and my friend had decided to retire. It's all about leadership. What leaders value, say, and do shape the very culture and life of the school, the power the school staff believes they have to engage in professional learning, and the values that undergird the work of every single teacher and staff member.

ASSUMPTIONS

- Highly effective leaders are model learners.
- They have an intense and unwavering focus on student learning.
- They have high regard for learning time for students, themselves, and the staff, and they maximize schedules to ensure adequate time.
- They build a shared vision that drives school planning and professional learning.
- They establish sustainable systems that induct new members, monitor practice, hold up the team's values and vision to be visible to all, and celebrate successes.
- They share leadership responsibilities easily with others throughout the organization. They honor the leadership efforts of others and nurture leadership development in teachers.
- Highly effective principals have a deep understanding of professional learning and the processes that focus the community on high-yield strategies.
- They build a community that values and engages in collaboration to increase the effectiveness of everyone and the success of students.
- They build energy in their organizations and honor the efforts of others through celebrations, storytelling, and acknowledging others' contributions.
- They stay focused on a goal, a process, or a system until all staff members use the process authentically and effectively.

REVIEW OF THE LITERATURE

Much has been written about school leadership and what matters. Hirsh and Killion (2007) summarized the findings in both research on highly effective principals and research on leadership in any organization:

> Leaders lead learning and share responsibility for leading. They model learning and shape the organization's culture so that it supports learning.

They share responsibility for learning and leading and they ensure the system is learning. They coach others toward excellence, they provide resources, they hold a vision of success and high expectations, and they build trusting relationships and lead with influence rather than coercion. Finally, they hold learning among their top priorities and allocate time and resources to it. (p. 39)

Internal Compass

I have observed other distinguishing characteristics. Highly effective principals hold true to their internal compass. They know who they are as people and as school principals. They are not overly worried about their role as principals as they see their work as only one aspect of their life. Consequently, they do not live in fear of what others think of them or of losing their jobs. They stay focused on the goals of the school in difficult, high-stress situations. They are confident that they and their school can accomplish whatever they set out to accomplish together. They commit to stay in the school long enough to see the vision become a reality. They do not have inflated egos or have to be the center of attention. They do not take credit! They are calm, confident, and reassuring. They live in lightness and gratitude for their opportunity to serve. One of my favorite books on leadership is Dennis Perkins et al.'s (2000) *Leading at the Edge: Leadership Lessons From the Extraordinary Saga of Shackleton's Antarctic Expedition.* The authors attribute Shackleton's leadership with everyone on the expedition making it safely home after the ship became frozen in the Antarctic ice. At one point, everyone was working extremely hard and one of the crewmembers lost his glove. Shackleton, who was working side by side with his men, took off his glove and gave it to his crewmember. Like Shackleton, principals and teacher leaders know who they are and live in gratitude that they have the opportunity to serve others.

Vision and Values

Highly effective principals continuously articulate their personal vision and values in all that they do. Sergiovanni (1992) states, "The heart of leadership has to do with what a person believes, values, and hopes for and is committed to" (p. 7). You often overhear these leaders in conversations with others, weaving the schools' and their personal vision and values through problem solving, celebrations, professional conversations, and learning experiences:

> I've been thinking, if we are really true to our vision. . . . Now how does that help us achieve what we said we need to accomplish? Is that in line with what we believe about children learning? How does this connect to what we are learning. . . .

These powerful principals know that the organization is continuously reshaped by their conversations. When people get off track and lose focus, these leaders redirect. When things are challenging, they inspire courage and confidence in others. Through their conversations, they remind people of what they are trying to accomplish together and they work to ensure that all members of the team share that vision and those values.

Furthermore, highly effective principals are not confined to the present structures. Though many people use the platitude, "If you do what you have always done, you will get what you have always got!" few really consider making major transformations of schools. Schools are organized very similarly to the way they have always been. Often, principals tell me that they cannot organize a schedule for common planning time. When I respond with, "Then why have a schedule—do away with it!" I get blank stares and brushed off. We all know that today we could create a world without poverty, without hunger, and without pollution to our environment, yet we do not reshape our work and world to do so. One of my most inspirational world leaders is Muhammad Yunus (2007), who received the Nobel Peace Prize in 2007 for his efforts to create social businesses—businesses in which stockholders do not receive dividends. Profits are used to achieve the mission and vision of the business. Through his leadership in innovative banking and his establishment of Grameen Bank in Bangladesh that gives small credit loans to women, he is leading Bangladesh to be the only nation to reach an national goal of reducing poverty to 50%. How could he have imagined such a thing? Poor people, especially women in Bangladesh, will not repay loans! And yet, he has a 99% payback record. Highly effective principals think like Yunus. They do not see current structures as barriers to achieving their mission. If they need to shift the schedule or do away with it, they do. If teams need time for lesson study, they find it. If students need to be more engaged in their own learning, they work with teachers to achieve the goal.

Intense Focus on Learning That Counts

Thomasina Piercy (2006), in *Compelling Conversations,* knew what was important and everything she did reflected her intense focus on student outcomes. She hosted regular conversations with each of her teachers concerning each student's achievement. She skillfully inquired as to which strategies were working and which were not. She never veered from her focus of increasing student performance one student at a time. Not only do these highly effective principals monitor student learning regularly with their team, they know what types of professional learning matters in the long run. They are not blown by the winds of innovation. They know that if the school family is focused on curriculum, instruction, and assessment work and their conversations are about the impact of that work on student work, students and staff will be learning. They are not drawn away from the heart work of the school by multiple, often conflicting programs that have little impact and drain energy. While other principals are enticed by what Hirsh and Killion (2007) call *the Christmas tree effect,* these principals stay intensely focused. According to Hirsh and Killion, schools are often weighted down with programs that are incoherent, disconnected, and sometimes even counter to each other like ornaments on a Christmas tree. Though the tree is standing, its roots are not being fed. It looks really good, but it is dead! I do not know how many schools I have encountered that are cluttered and overburdened with programs, new materials, and activities that will not yield greater results in student learning but that drain energy from the staff. Highly effective principals know how to feed the very roots of the school. They stay focused on the school's vision, on intense professional conversations, and on learning strategies that yield the greatest results. They ward off those who wish to entice them into implementation of programs that will divert their attention and consume time and energy needed for teams to focus on student outcomes. Long-term, intensive focus facilitates building sustained change.

Presence

A good leader's very presence is inspirational. I am not talking charismatic; I am talking "energy full." Leaders are aware that they are a source of energy and inspiration. The entire school community sees them as visionary, trustworthy, optimistic, courageous, and reliable. Their presences build a pervasive mood in their organizations that the school family can do anything together. They are visible. When they are in the building, they are with teams of teachers. They participate in walk-throughs, they lead lesson studies, they engage in coaching, and they do model lessons. They understand that if they are going to be the model of what they want to see in others, they must spend time drafting curriculum maps with teams, they must design assessments, and they must engage in analysis of student work. They do not get caught in the trap of not getting out of their office or putting out fires. They put first things first, as Covey (2005) would say!

A Mood of Optimism

I once was amazed by a conversation I witnessed when superintendents were talking about the challenges they face in hiring highly effective principals. It led to a conversation among several superintendents concerning the difficulty districts were having in finding outstanding superintendents. Several were talking about the lack of interest among teachers to become principals and the lack of interest among principals in becoming superintendents. One person stated, "Maybe we do not inspire our principals to become superintendents because we never tell them about the joy in our work." Another spoke up, "Well, I don't know what the joys are; they need to know just how difficult and challenging this work really is!" Everyone grew quiet. Finally, a third reflected, "Maybe through the press and media, they already know how challenging the work is; maybe they do not know the vision we have for our schools and the passion we have for our work." Highly effective leaders share their passions and their optimism for their work. They share stories and metaphors of powerful teams. Their compelling messages, tone, and energy engage and infect others. Over time, all begin to see themselves as part of a powerful, winning team.

The Skills of Collaboration, Persistence, Leadership Development, and Celebration Are Essential to Sustaining Change

Most important, these highly effective principals view themselves as one of the team. They are not hungry for power; they do not need their egos fed. They are not coercive and controlling. Meg Wheatley (1992), in her book *Leading and the New Science*, said it best:

> In life, the issue is not control, but dynamic connectedness (Jantsch, 1980). If we believe that acting responsibly means exerting control by having our hands into everything, then we cannot hope for anything except what we already have—a treadmill of effort and life-destroying stress. (p. 23)

Powerful principals keep energy high by engaging everyone in the work, making learning the norm, and recognizing outstanding efforts. They inspire continuous learning among everyone in the organization. Continuous learning sustains the school's efforts. They celebrate short-term wins and highlight teams that are being successful. They are in tune with the energy level in the organization and intuitively know when to refocus, when to intensify the work, and how to harness positive energy among the staff (Loehr & Schwartz, 2003). When faced with resistance, the school leaders ask, under what conditions can we make this work? They listen intently to every viewpoint and consider thoughtful ideas. They slow down. They invite others to research and explore, and they ensure everyone that, in the end, they will make decisions together that are in the best interest of students. And they mean it!

Building a deep bench of leaders is essential to sustaining a school's efforts. These highly skilled principals take seriously their role in developing leaders. They engage many members of the staff in leadership responsibilities. They do not delegate tasks for others to do; they develop leaders (Ackerman & Mackenzie, 2007; Killion & Harrison, 2006; Lambert, 1998). In schools with highly effective principals, team leaders are guiding teams in establishing walkthroughs or lesson studies. Grade levels or course leaders are leading conversations around curriculum with other grade levels. Veteran teachers are coaching new teachers to be successful and inducting them into the values and behaviors of a professional learning community. Most important, these principals never give up. They affirm a belief that they look forward to success and take every setback as temporary.

Learning communities sustain change. Learning is changing behavior (Senge, 2000). The challenge for principals is to ensure that everyone in the organization is learning every day. The principals use powerful school-planning systems that engage the school staff in exploring new innovations to impact student learning, and they work over several years to ensure their full implementation. These leaders have a deep understanding of change and have a theory of change that leads to success for all (Hord & Sommers, 2008). They continuously engage everyone in developing clarity of the vision, the power of a learning community, and the progress the school is making. They continue to focus the team on embedding these new practices into "the way we are."

Powerful principals engage all in the conversations of the heart. They inspire the community by reminding everyone that their work matters; it's a value to students and our society. Over time, teams begin to realize how much they are learning through collaboration and how successful they are becoming. Because a large part of the team's learning time is time within the school day, the staff members begin to see their learning as essential to their work, a natural part of their work, an essential part of their work. They share what they are doing publicly. They present at conferences, write articles, host teacher-led, schoolwide conferences to share and celebrate their work and what they are learning. They own the changes in themselves, grow confident in their skills to learn together and to facilitate student learning, respect the community, and enjoy the journey of leading and learning.

District Responsibility

Tom Many and Dennis King (2008), in the article "Districts Speak with One Voice," share the vital roles district leaders play in sustaining efforts. They state that for schools to be successful, districts must have a shared vision and an intensive focus on student outcomes. To sustain their efforts to transform their schools into professional learning communities, the districts featured in the article modeled what they wanted to see in schools: an intense focus on student learning, fewer goals and long-term focus on them, a movement away from training to learning through team development of curriculum maps and common assessments, a collaborative culture that is "relentlessly restless," and continuous conversations among district administrators and school principals about progress. This intensive long-term focus led the districts to greater success.

In implementing the processes for learning recommended in this book, Lin Reeves, superintendent of North Marion School District in Aurora, Oregon, worked with the community and school board to develop a shared vision for their district through their strategic planning process. Teacher leaders, principals, school board members, and community members worked together to establish clear goals and researched processes to increase students and staff success. Though there was training and facilitation for staff members to design common curriculum maps, assessments, and instructional plans, principals and teacher leaders at each school played a major role in "seeing it through"—renewing the focus, energizing staff, reflecting on the work, and celebrating and sustaining the effort. Principals and teachers reflected higher energy and passion in the school for their work. They shared that the communities are learning to work together, are building trust in one another, and are more successful with all students.

District superintendents and school boards also play a major role in sustaining district efforts and achieving district goals through the decisions they make when hiring principals and superintendents. District superintendents and school boards who are most successful develop open, trusting relationships. They take their hiring practices very seriously. They design logical, effective strategies for leadership succession that will keep the district focused and continuing on its journey of learning. If the district has shared values and vision and intensive strategies for success toward building professional learning communities, people in the school district are developing leadership skills. Though not everyone has the strengths or interest in leadership essential to lead an organization, those who do, need to have the opportunity to become principals and superintendents in their own districts. Of course, at times, new people bring fresh, new ideas and energy to an organization, but these new people are most successful when they understand the culture, values, mission, vision, and goals of the district and are hired to continue the work. Continuous shifts in focus are disastrous for schools. "This year's new thing" or "I wonder what new initiatives this superintendent will bring" smothers sustaining efforts over time. When districts develop leadership succession plans, they capitalize on the investments in people that the district has been making to build professional learning communities.

They Count It All Joy!

In his book, *Leadership,* Rudolph Guiliani (2002) shares his stories and personal struggles shortly after 9/11 and the fall of the Twin Towers. He sat alone in his office trying to determine what he could have done to prevent this heinous tragedy. After a while of trying to diagnose what went wrong and what he could have done to prevent this catastrophe, he began to realize the needs of the world and especially the American people at this time. He moved from blaming himself and others to inspiration, and none will forget his words. His comments lifted spirits in the midst of great loss:

> This was not just an attack on the city of New York or on the United States of America. It was an attack on the very idea of a free, inclusive, and civil society. . . . This massive attack was intended to break our spirit. It has not done that. It has made us stronger, more determined, and more resolved. . . . The best long-term deterrent to terrorism is the spread of our principles of freedom, democracy, the rule of law, and the respect for human life. . . . Once these ideals gain a foothold, they cannot be stopped. (p. 184–187)

Great principals are empathetic toward the daily challenges and sometimes horrific conditions in which their students live, but they have great faith that through meaningful relationships with adults and rigorous, challenging curriculum experiences, all students will have purposeful options for their lives and hopes for their futures. Regardless of the political winds shaking public education, they stay focused and committed to building learning organizations. Even in the most stressful of situations, powerful principals move all toward optimism and hope!

FOCUS QUESTIONS

- What do highly effective principals do to lead their school community to become an intensely focused, powerful professional learning community?
- Which strategies do these principals use to build leadership throughout the organization?
- How do teacher leaders model and facilitate learning in the community?

THE VISION

The school principal and the leadership team guide the entire staff to develop an intense focus on learning. They lead the staff to declare the assumptions that all students can learn whatever is expected in the curriculum and that they control the conditions for success. The leadership team guides others to develop a shared and compelling vision for the school and establishes a clear plan of action to achieve it. They monitor continuously the progress of every child. They continuously seek new and innovative strategies for intervening when students and staff are not finding success. The leadership team takes every opportunity to model and lead others to reflective practices and to monitor progress. They insure that learning is embedded into the daily life of the school for everyone and that their learning has significant impact on student learning. Through sharing stories and engaging in ceremonies, they lead celebrations that build a culture of learning, sustaining change, and achieving goals.

Figure 9.1 Comparing Traditional Approaches to Professional Learning With the Professional Learning Community

Traditional Perspectives	Professional Learning Communities
• All view the principal as a building manager. • Teachers have little involvement in leadership in the school. • Those in the school, including the principal, work in isolation. • The principal is often in his or her office "putting out fires" and managing student discipline. • The staff wants students to be successful but believes that the burden rests with students.	• The principal is viewed as a facilitator and model of learning in the organization. • The principal sets the expectations that all will learn continuously and work collaboratively to focus on student outcomes. • Teacher leadership emerges throughout the organization; some lead study groups, others lead grade levels or course teams in designing curriculum maps and common assessments; some induct new staff members; some serve on the school leadership team, insuring analysis of student performance data, effective planning, and full implementation of agreed upon innovations. • The principal and leadership team sustain change by ensuring that everyone in the organization is learning. They ground all innovation in a theory of change and develop a logical process for achieving goals that makes sense to everyone. They see the change process through until all in the organization are systematically using the strategies effectively. • The leadership team hosts regular celebrations of progress toward achieving the vision and goals of the school and to recognize staff for their contributions. The team makes modifications when things are not working well. • The principal hosts regular conversations with other principals and central staff about progress in achieving the district and school goals. • Districts develop leadership-development and succession plans to ensure a strong pipeline of leaders who have the values, skills, attitudes, and aspirations of the district and a commitment to the district's innovations.

CHALLENGE STRATEGIES

1. If you are a principal, reflect on your own assumptions about leading schools to high performance, professional learning, and student achievement. Write down your assumptions. Reflect on how these assumptions guide your actions. Think about how these assumptions facilitate your school in becoming a learning community and how some of them prevent you from leading.

2. If you are a member of the school leadership team or wish to become a teacher leader, engage in research and discovery about the essential skills, attitudes, behaviors, and aspirations of teacher leaders. Many resources are available to assist you. Several are listed in the resources.

3. Establish a vision and clearly defined assumptions of the role of leaders who lead effective learning organizations. Discuss this vision and these assumptions with all in the school. Reflect on their feedback to make essential revisions in your work. Live by them.

4. Immerse yourself and your leadership team in developing a deep understanding of theories of change and developing sustainable systems. Develop a theory of change around the strategies recommended in this book. There are many resources to assist you. Too many schools today begin innovations that are never fully implemented. Leaders see change through to full fruition.

5. Seek examples of highly effective principals and teacher leaders and visit their schools. Interview them. Host focus groups with teachers to discern the distinct roles these individuals play and the skills they have in leading their schools to high performance.

6. Conduct a self-evaluation based upon what you have learned, and set goals for yourself to increase your effectiveness. Seek a peer to coach you and give you feedback as you work to achieve your goals.

7. Seek feedback from the staff to determine your progress.

TWO STORIES

These two stories are not about specific principals, but a compilation of principals who have either been most successful or who have actually been barriers to their staff becoming a professional community of learners.

It's All About Me! I Am the Leader!

It's all about me struggles continuously to allow leadership to emerge throughout the organization. The notion that "I am in control! The buck stops here!" interferes with this principal's or teacher leader's ability to allow others to lead. When teams are creative and begin a learning journey, their efforts are often stifled due to lack of learning on the part of the principal or the teacher leaders. *It's all about me* often refers to those he or she works with as theirs—*my* students, *my* faculty, *my* school. *It's all about mes* equate their role with their status in the organization; therefore, any achievement gains are a direct result of the leader. When things do not go well, they find ways to blame, belittle, and put down others in order to divert attention from the leadership. *It's all about me* may say things like, "The central office does not give me enough resources to . . ." or, "The staff will not . . ." or, "Those students just will not. . . ." Staff perceive these leaders as the decision makers, and they wait for direction. When things do not go well, they blame the school leadership. Instead of a sense of community, under *It's all about me,* teachers and principals work in isolation. Small groups often form around issues. The emergent culture is one of stress and tension.

We Can Do Anything, Together!

When someone walks into the community of learners, the principal *We can do anything, together* has pictures of staff members and teams with their contributions to the mission in the entry way. The hallways are full of student work and student recognitions, pictures of students engaged in learning, and pictures of parent nights. The vision and values of the school are woven into and become real in the stories of student and staff achievements on the walls.

There is a hum of excitement and high energy. Teams of students are everywhere—the library, the office, the classrooms, the cafeterias, or outside in the outdoor learning centers. Sometimes it is difficult to recognize the teacher in a classroom of students. There are no classrooms in which desks are in rows facing the teacher. Students are meaningfully engaged in work with others, using computers, conducting research, building projects, or making presentations to share their findings. They are sitting in small groups reading to each other, problem solving, and debating issues.

The leadership team meetings and agendas are posted. Staff meetings are filled with teacher teams sharing and problem solving, with collaboration and celebration. There are feelings of optimism, pride, fun, and confidence among staff members. In most staff meetings, the principal is sitting at one of the tables learning from those leading the session. The data team is assisting all team members in understanding how well students are doing. Other teachers are guiding the staff through a six-traits scoring rubric and using models of their students' work to show high-quality writing at each grade level. This group of teacher leaders then guides the group through problem-solving strategies at their grade level to increase effectiveness in teaching students to write. The mathematics team is hosting afterschool sessions on mathematical reasoning. Several teams are attending and using what they are learning during their planning time to plan mathematical instruction.

One *We can do anything, together* principal shared with me that the teachers began to debate the most effective strategies for teaching students phonics. The debate went on for some time. Each team had their research to support their position. The principal simply suggested that each team engage in action research. He said:

> I could have stepped in and given them my opinion and that might have stopped the debate; however, I want the debate to continue. I want them to be in control of their decisions and to use research-based professional learning strategies to determine the outcome.

Another shared that her retirement party was on the last professional-development day on the calendar before school ended. They had a wonderful party to start the day, and the learning community presented her with a wonderful scrapbook of their learning journey together. As soon as the social ended and the tables cleared, every community started work on revising their curriculum maps and their assessments to start the next year. She was thrilled, "I can retire; the work will go on; the community is theirs, and they are confident that their working together is what counts!"

IN SUMMARY

When leaders are the models they want to see in others, everyone in the school accelerates their learning. As principals and teacher leaders collaborate effectively to achieve a shared vision, others collaborate effectively. When leaders host valid, authentic conversations about student learning, others become inquisitive. Effective school leaders value their role in developing leadership in others and in facilitating professional learning. They build leaders throughout the organization. While they are the guardians of the vision, they lead everyone to share that vision and work hard to achieve it. The powerful leaders in schools consider themselves lead learners and are not afraid to take risks and try new strategies if there is hope that these strategies will yield greater results. They are systems-thinkers and ground their leadership in theories of change that sustain innovation and lead to authentic change. These powerful leaders are continuously aware of the energy level and work systematically to ensure everyone is learning. Finally, they know the value of shared leadership. As they share leadership responsibilities with others, leadership flourishes throughout the organization.

REFLECTIVE QUESTIONS

- Which personal attitudes, behaviors, and assumption do I have that facilitate my development and nurturing of a professional learning community?
- What do I need to learn to be more effective in leading a professional learning community? What strategies will best facilitate my learning? How will I monitor and measure my progress?
- What is *systems-thinking*? What do we mean by a *theory of change*? How do schools and organizations develop logic models, innovation configurations, and school-planning systems to lead and sustain change? What barriers will I face in achieving my goal? How will I overcome those barriers? What are our best strategies for celebrating our successes?
- What resources will I need to be successful?

EXTENDED LEARNING OPPORTUNITIES

1. Establish a study group of principals or teacher leaders to research effective leadership strategies and skills essential to developing professional learning communities.

2. Set goals for yourselves and work with your study team or a peer to encourage and support you in your efforts and to problem solve when things do not seem to be going well.

3. Seek a professional coach to guide you on your leadership development journey.

Resources

RESOURCE A

Our Assumptions About Student and Staff Learning

Many assumptions open up opportunities for us to learn together. We enjoy celebrating our students' successes. We believe we make a difference in the world, so we are proud to be teachers. Just as some of our assumptions open up opportunities, some prevent us from making essential shifts in our thinking and actions that would facilitate all children learning.

What do we really believe about student learning? Do our assumptions facilitate us holding expectations high for all children and ensuring their success in the world, or are there powerful beliefs that are actually barriers to our success with every child?

For example, some of us might hold the assumption that all children can learn anything that intrigues them and that they have the courage to learn. How would such a belief open doors for all of us?

What are your assumptions about student learning? Are they generative for you as a teacher?

Some of us may hold an assumption that professional development really does not impact teacher behaviors or attitudes, nor does it positively impact student learning. What doors does this belief close for us?

What assumptions about professional learning, if we held them, would generate new possibilities for us?

Write your assumptions clearly before attending our session on _____. Be ready to share your thinking.

RESOURCE B

The Principles of Professional Learning

Principle 1: Principles

Principles shape our thoughts, words, and actions.

Principle 2: Diversity

Diversity strengthens an organization and improves its decisions.

Principle 3: Leadership

Leaders are responsible for building the capacity in individuals, teams, and organizations to be leaders and learners.

Principle 4: Planning

Ambitious goals lead to powerful actions and remarkable results.

Principle 5: Focus

Focusing professional learning on teaching and student learning produces academic success.

Principle 6: Impact

Evaluation strengthens performance and results.

Principle 7: Expertise

Communities can solve even their most complex problems by tapping internal expertise.

Principal 8: Collaboration

Collaboration among educators builds shared responsibility and improves student learning.

Source: Hirsh, S., & Killion, J. (2007). *The Learning Educator.* Oxford, OH: National Staff Development Council.

RESOURCE C

Our Vision of Our School
Iduma Elementary School
Killeen ISD
Killeen, TX

Everyone in the school community is energized by and passionate about achieving our mission. We have a deep understanding of the challenges facing our school community, and everyone contributes continuously.

We are a fun loving, collaborative, focused, enthusiastic, risk-taking, intelligent community of learners with a reputation for excellence.

Students engage in learning what is meaningful to them and make significant progress in achieving state and national standards. They value learning; they respect themselves and others; they share in the responsibility of a democratic school in which all achieve at high levels.

Staff members engage in continuous learning. We use research and data to guide our decisions. We support each other and mentor each other so that all are highly competent. We share the responsibility for all students in the school and acknowledge our power and control to change those aspects of the school that have the greatest impact on student learning. We meaningfully engage students, parents, and community members in understanding the learning process, the expectations for student success, and ways they can powerfully partner with us.

Parents and community members engage as equal partners in ensuring the success of all students. They make positive contributions at school, in their businesses and places of community service, and at home to ensure students are healthy and engaged in learning.

RESOURCE D

A Learning Walk

Planning for Our Walk

- What are our guiding principles or assumptions?
- What is our vision?
- What would we expect to see students, staff, parents, principals, and school leaders doing if we were living our vision?

Designing Our Tools and Our Process

- Who will walk where? When?
- How will we record our observations? What charts will we use?

What Conversations Will We Host After Our Learning Walk?

- What did we see that was aligned with our vision and our assumptions?
- How often did we see aligned behavior and attitudes?
- What unique observations did we make about students? Staff? Parents? Principals? School leaders?
- What strengths did we discover? What celebrations do we want to host?
- What challenges do we face? What next steps might we take?
- How will we record our conversation to share with others?

What Conversations Do We Want to Host With Others? Students? Parents? The Entire Faculty?

- Who will host these conversations? When? Where?
- What will be the purpose of them?
- What will we do as a result?

For more information on conducting walkthroughs, see Chapter 8, "Conducting Classroom Walkthroughs" in Easton's (2008) book *Powerful Designs for Professional Learning.*

RESOURCE E

We Are a School Community
That Values Learning

We Are Models of What We Want to See in Our Students:

A Prompt for Beginning a Conversation About the
School Community's Vision of Itself as a Community of Learners

In our school, students

- are intrigued by learning,
- engage in the life of the school,
- value their relationships with their peers and the adults in the school,
- are mindful of their learning, and
- are critical and reflective thinkers.

Teachers

- collaborate with one another to reflect on their work, to encourage each other, and to learn together;
- engage in meaningful dialogue around the concepts and standards to be learned by students;
- expect the best from every student; and
- engage in a lesson study, book studies, and tuning protocols to implement innovative instructional strategies and analyze student work.

Administrators

- are model learners,
- help to make the learning community's vision clear to everyone,
- nurture learning throughout the organization, and
- encourage and celebrate effort and achievement.

Support staff are

Parents are

Community members are

RESOURCE F

Our Learning Community's Norms

We Are a Highly Skilled and Productive Team Because
We Live by the Following Norms

- All members of our team will be present at every meeting, on time, with assignments completed.
- We will meet to share ideas, design assessments, revise our curriculum maps, and/or analyze student work three times a week.
- We make important decisions by consensus.
- When strong and disruptive disagreements occur, we will ask a facilitator to mediate our conversations so that we maintain trust and open communication.
- We will stay focused on our agenda and achieve our goals together.
- Learning together is our primary agenda item at every meeting.

RESOURCE G

Quakertown High School Goals

	LONG-TERM OUTCOME: All students improve significantly their performance on standards.	INTERMEDIATE GOALS	SHORT-TERM GOALS
CURRICULUM	• Teacher-developed curricula are based on district-adopted standards that are 　○ clearly stated, 　○ measurable, and 　○ known and understood by students, parents, staff, and community. • Students communicate their understanding of the standards through their application and modeling. 　○ Students apply and model standards in their work. 　○ Students use reading and writing strategies to learn content. • The curricula include a variety of real-world and current resources.	• All high school curricula are revised to include standards, essential understanding and essential questions based on the district's curriculum-management system. • Daily instruction focuses on ensuring that students know the connection between the instruction in the classroom and the standards. • Teachers receive training and coaching on using reading and writing strategies to support student success on the high school curriculum standards.	• The teacher leadership team will practice, implement, and reflect on its use of curriculum standards to drive their instruction and assessment of student learning. • They will share their learning experiences with colleagues in the high school. • The leadership will work to define *constructivist*.
INSTRUCTION	• Instruction 　○ engages students in meaningful, authentic work that is based on the standards; 　○ engages students in conversations about the enduring understanding and essential questions that have emerged from the standards; 　○ is purposeful, researched based, and uses a variety of strategies; 　○ is fundamentally constructivist; 　○ engages learners in reflective practice and revision; 　○ builds on prior knowledge; and 　○ establishes norms necessary for successful learning.	• Teachers organize lessons that focus on standards, engage students in dialogue and conversation, as well as collaboration, and problem solving based on the essential questions. • Teachers use instructional strategies that are shown by research to be effective in improving student performance. • Instruction engages students in authentic work.	• The teacher leadership team engages in purposeful application of research-based instructional strategies. • The teacher leadership team members observe each other and give each other feedback about the effectiveness of their instructional strategies. • The leadership team invites critical friends to join in the practice of purposeful application, observation, and feedback. • The leadership team will work to define *inquiry*.

(Continued)

(Continued)

LONG-TERM OUTCOME: All students improve significantly their performance on standards.	INTERMEDIATE GOALS	SHORT-TERM GOALS
ASSESSMENT • Assessments are aligned with standards and are designed prior to instruction. • Teachers work collaboratively to develop and revise common assessments. • Teachers use assessment data to adjust instructional units and plans. • Teachers measure students' performance to see if they meet standard. • Assessment is an instructional tool. • Teacher use data to group and regroup students and to extend learning opportunity.	• Teachers working collaboratively experiment with an array of assessment strategies that are aligned with standards. • Common assessments are produced and shared with students prior to instruction. • Teachers use data to reflect and revise their practice and extend learning opportunities for students. • Teachers use models and student work to assist students with revisions prior to final grading.	• The teacher leadership team plans assessment collaboration with the general teaching body. • The teacher leadership team develops examples of assessments that are aligned with standards. • The leadership team displays and models standards-based assessment tools including student work. • Colleagues are invited to join in the development of common assessments to enhance the quality of those assessments.
REFLECTION • Students accept the responsibility for their own learning, reflect regularly on what they are learning and pursue personal goals to produce higher quality work. • Teachers use student data to inform their work with students.	• Teachers use assessment data to revise and adjust instruction. • Teachers provide opportunities for students to reflect on their learning. • Reflection and debriefing occur through a variety of specific strategies. • Teachers use student reflection to assess instruction. • Teachers use student reflection to assess student achievement. • Students reflect regularly on what they are learning. • Teachers model reflection strategies for students.	• The leadership team Investigates and shares other ideas on the topic of reflection. • The leadership team uses reflection strategies in their implementation of best practices. • The leadership team members share their their reflections about their their individual implementation efforts with the team.

	LONG-TERM OUTCOME: All students improve significantly their performance on standards.	INTERMEDIATE GOALS	SHORT-TERM GOALS
COLLABORATION	• Teams of teachers work collaboratively on curriculum to o make revisions, o keep resources current, and o refine essential questions and enduring understandings. • Students collaborate on authentic content issues that engage them in deeper understandings of the concepts and standards of the curricula. • Students and staff assist each other through peer coaching, evaluation, and problem solving. • Teachers model collaboration for students.	• Departments select and develop exemplars for students to use as models to increase their success. • Teams of teachers collaboratively begin to create a system to revise, review, modify, and update current resource. • Teachers and students will continue to explore real-world issues to enhance essential concepts and curricula. • Teachers and students will use skills to assist in learning.	• Teachers work collaboratively to develop curriculum using enduring understandings and essential questions. • Teachers and students will collaboratively define real-world issues in order to set the path for deeper understanding. • Teachers and students will learn skills for collaboration.
PHYSICAL ENVIRONMENT	• The classroom is a showcase of exemplary student work to accelerate the learning of all students. • The classroom is an environment that o is conducive to student collaboration and o encourages meaningful learning. • A designated staff location is provided for curricular collaboration. • Time is formally provided for staff collaboration.	• Teachers use exemplary student work as a guide for instruction. • Teachers teach skills necessary for collaboration and meaningful learning. • Staff is assigned to departmentalized sections. • Staff development schedule is examined and revised to accommodate whole-school and district collaboration.	• Teachers define exemplary work, and examples are collected. • Teachers research and develop skills necessary for collaboration and meaningful learning. • Teachers explore possibilities of room utilization. • Teachers explore possibilities of options for common planning time.

RESOURCE H

Example Letter to Parents

Dear Parents,

We are excited about the beginning of a new school year. I am most happy that your student is taking _____ or is in my class.

The high school Freshman English I teaching team wants to share with you what your students will be learning this year.

The essential standards (skills students are expected to know well) are

We also want them to be good thinkers, creative problem solvers, and good citizens in our school and in our community. Therefore, we are also going to be sure that they are self directed learners who work well with others, respect others, and give their best effort. Therefore, we will be using a variety of instructional strategies that will guide your student to problem solve, use technology, write for a variety of purposes, and read a variety of printed materials.

We will be hosting several parent nights this year for your students to explain what they are learning. Those dates are

When we see you on "Back to School Night" on_____, at _____, we will share with you our grading practices so you know how your student will be graded. We will also show you several examples of work of students who have taken our course before so that you will have an idea of the quality of work expected.

We know it is going to be a great year! We will send a similar letter to this one home each grading period so that you will know the standards expected each term. We know you are concerned about your student's success in school. All of us, your student, you, and this team, will do all we can to ensure your student's learning.

Sincerely,

RESOURCE I

Critical Attributes of a Performance Task or Project

Description: Students are asked to work alone or with others to produce an artifact that reflects proficiency of the standards and concepts for a unit of study. It may be a performance, a project, a debate, a speech, a simulation, a piece of writing, or a combination of these.

Critical Attributes:

The performance task project

Content

- clearly and authentically assesses the standards and concepts to be learned;
- expects students to create, produce, explain, analyze, justify, share, and reflect;
- expects students to apply standards and concepts intentionally in settings, strategies, or models that would mirror the use of these skills and thinking in the world outside of school;
- is grounded in accurate information and data; and
- uses reliable sources.

Process

- is woven throughout instruction, with students completing components at established checkpoints throughout the unit;
- is valued by the students, who find meaning, interest, and purpose in the work;
- expects students to self-reflect, analyze learnings, and establish purposeful goals for themselves;
- is intriguing to other students and elicits dialogue and discussion; and
- is a sane thing to do—the value of doing the work to the learning is worth the investment of time.

Product

- is professional, polished, novel, and organized in a way that attracts attention from others;
- makes the learnings clearly evident; and
- is the original work by students.

Note: The authentic performance task or project is not a homework assignment.

RESOURCE J

Template for Culminating Demonstrations

Critical Attributes:

Limitations:

Task Analysis:

What must the students **analyze**?	What must the students **apply**?	What must the students **synthesize**?	What must the students **evaluate**?
Which new **concepts** do students need to know?	Which **vocabulary** is essential?	Which **terms** are essential?	Which **processes** must students use?

RESOURCE K

Example of a Second-Grade, First-Term Culminating Demonstration

Essential Question for the Term:

How do we positively contribute to our community?

Description of Culminating Demonstrations:

Students will design a classroom book to be our classroom constitution, and they will host an effective class meeting, role playing behaviors that are appropriate according to our constitution prior to this culminating demonstration. In their meeting, students will reference our class book, *Our Classroom Constitution*, concerning behavior in the classroom.

Classroom Demonstration I: A Classroom Meeting

We, as a class, are having several issues or may have certain issues come up that we will want to solve. Let's generate what we think these issues might be. You will role play a class meeting concerning the issue your team draws. Your team will model multiple ways the class could solve this problem. Be sure to reference our class book, Our Classroom Constitution.

Critical Attributes:

- Each person on a team will play a role in the issue that the team is working on. Each team will establish their team's own roles.
- The team in its role playing must generate several ways the class could solve the problem and share their ideas about which strategies might be best.
- The team must stay on topic, reference the class book, and justify an appropriate solution.

Limitation:

- There will be no name calling or making fun of others.

Task Analysis:

What Must the Students *Analyze?*	What Must the Student *Apply?*	What Must the Student *Synthesize?*	What Must the Students *Evaluate?*
Students must compare and contrast behaviors that align with the Classroom Constitution and behaviors that do not.	Students must use their skills of staying focused on a topic and staying in their roles.	Students must generate multiple ways, that are aligned with the Classroom Constitution, to solve problems that arise in the classroom.	Students must distinguish appropriate behavior and judge the most effective strategies for resolving the issue.

(Continued)

(Continued)

Which New **Concepts** Do Students Need to Know?	Which **Vocabulary Words** Are Essential?	Which **Terms** Are Essential?	Which **Processes** Must Students Use?
Communities are more harmonious and successful when they agree on a set of rules and follow those rules.	Community Appropriate Behavior Responsibility Contribution	Constitution Collaboration Democracy	Collaboration Problem solving Role playing

RESOURCE L

Example of a Second-Grade, Third-Term Culminating Demonstrations

Essential Question for the Term:

How do we creatively express ourselves to inspire, contribute, and influence the thinking of others?

Standards (From the Map for the Third Term)

Social Studies	Describes/depicts calendar-time sequences and chronological sequences with narratives.
Science	Uses scientific process and is able to identify, describe, analyze, and interpret daily events.
Reading	Uses decoding and word-recognition skills to read a variety of texts, and understands common abbreviations and uses knowledge of individual words to predict meaning of compound words.
Writing	Writes biography, autobiography, and expository text including multi-step instructions and letter writing; uses writing process; uses transitions and transitional words (first, next, then, after); and writes using appropriate abbreviations, contractions; and capitalizations (for greetings, titles, initials, etc.).
Oral Language	Focuses on language structures and patterns through songs, chants, rhymes, and stories; has fun with words; makes links between oral and written language; engages in small- and large-group language-development opportunities; learns through speaking, listening, exploring, and collaboration; distinguishes between author's purpose, audience; and listens to others actively and critically and responds appropriately.
Art	Responds to different works of art, identifies events and conditions that inspire works of art, creates art to achieve desired affect, and communicate verbally and in writing in simple vocabulary regarding various works of art.
Collaboration with others	Treats each other with respect at all times; solves problems in the best interest of the team; persists through issues to achieve goals; and enjoys the diversity of languages, ideas, and children in the classroom.
Thinks deeply	Constantly explores ideas to answer the essential question.

Description of Culminating Demonstrations:

Students will organize and host a festival celebrating the arts. Students will express themselves through the arts utilizing the community as a resource.

(Continued)

(Continued)

Classroom Demonstration: A Village Art Festival

As a class, we are hosting a village art festival to share with our community how we as artists and how other artists from around the world and from our community inspire, contribute, and influence the thinking of others.

In order to prepare for our festival, we will study different forms of art. We will produce art ourselves. Then we will design a festival, inviting family, friends, and community members to experience art with us.

Critical Attributes:

- Student may imitate and/or create works of art in the style of established artists or writers.
- Students will select an area of art of interest to them offered by their teachers and specialize in that area to produce their art.
- Students will write a reflection of what they learned about the power of art and answer the inquiry question for the term.
- Students will study the life of an artist and write a biography of that person and how his/her art influenced others.
- All students in the grade level will host a grade-level meeting to design the art festival. They will interview local arts and ask them to respond to the inquiry question for the term. They will interview people in the community who regularly host art festivals to generate their plan.
- Students will attend a local art festival.
- Students will design a calendar of events to ensure everything is ready for the festival and to ensure all student artwork is shared.
- Students will collaborate to write a program, advertising, letters of invitation, and a newspaper article.

Limitation:

- There will be no artwork produced outside of class that will be shared in the festival.

Task Analysis:

What Must the Students *Analyze?*	What Must the Student *Apply?*	What Must the Student *Synthesize?*	What Must Students *Evaluate?*
Students must discern and describe the contribution of their chosen artists to the community. They must determine how art inspires, contributes, and influences others.	Students must use their oral and written language skills to write their chosen artists' biographies, their reflection pieces, and the text for the program, advertisements, letters of invitations, and newspaper articles.	Students must generate a plan and a timeline for the festival. They must produce a work of art. They must design a program and write a newspaper article and an invitation to their festival.	Students must judge the contributions of themselves and other artists to the world.

Which New **Concepts** Do Students Need to Know?	Which **Vocabulary Words** Are Essential?	Which **Terms** Are Essential?	Which **Processes** Must Students Use?
Art is powerful in that it inspires, challenges, and influences the thinking of others. Art tells a story and reflects a culture's values.	newspaper articles. Art Artist Festival Inspire Influence Style	Biography Terms are unique to the art form and will be determined by individual teachers.	Collaboration Problem solving Planning Writing (letter writing, newspaper article, program)

RESOURCE M

Precision in Adverbs

Rubrics are tools that allow staff and students to identify critical attributes and judge quality. High-quality rubrics rely on precise language. Avoid words that are unclear and vague, such as *some, most,* or *often*. Counting items is a reflection of neither an attribute nor quality. Having three inaccurate, unclear details is far less powerful than one thought-provoking detail. Some teams generate the critical attributes first and then begin to find the precise language needed to discern levels of quality. The following is a list of adverbs that may assist the team in working toward precise language. Use it as a starter if you wish for generating your own. Consider adverbs that reflect time, effort, accuracy, energy, organization, and presentation.

Exemplary	Proficiently (meets standard)	Emerging	Basic
Thoroughly	Efficiently	Inadequately	Inaccurately
Thoughtfully	Accurately	Infrequently	Unacceptably
Precisely	Clearly	Irregularly	Confusingly
Rigorously	Adequately	Inconsistently	Incorrectly
Creatively	Sufficiently	Intermittently	Improperly
Enthusiastically	Skillfully	Minimally	Unsatisfactorily
Passionately	Competently	Faultily	Perfunctorily
Eagerly	Graphically	Ineffectively	Unresponsively
Openly	Knowledgeably	Unemotionally	
Persistently	Consistently	Sporadically	
Elegantly	Continuously	Erratically	
Artistically	Objectively	Dispassionately	
Uniquely		Expressionlessly	
Expertly			
Ideally			
Emphatically			
Commendably			

RESOURCE N

Exemplary Rubric: Middle Ages Scoring Guide

---

1. Competent Communication: Speech, Journal, etc.

4- Persuasive: draws listener/reader in; clear; focused; interesting; memorable; elegant; verifiable; justifiable; supported with data and reliable sources; uses stories, narratives, powerful analogies; fluent
3- Informative: clear; focused; interesting; not overly persuasive/convincing; lacks passion
2- Confusing: unclear; incomplete; simplistic organization; restates verbatim
1- Incoherent: fragmented; pointless

---

2. *Homo Faber:* Student-Centered Creation (Some Kind of Creative Product)

4- Inventive: displays effort, thought, and creativity exemplified by being atypical, sophisticated, and reflecting student's uniqueness
3- Interpretive: displays some effort and thought; models; uses inferences; personalizes ideas, but not unique
2- Literal: displays little effort and thought; recreates existing models
1- Novice: displays bare minimum effort; unimaginative; last-minute quality

---

3. Critical Thinking: Bibliography, "Big Six," Venn Diagrams, Webbing, Journal, etc.

4- Mindful: uses a variety of strategies and sources to investigate; synthesizes collected information/research; use of graphic organizers to make significant connections with what they are learning about their world and their own lives; uses multiple strategies for solving problems; reflections show higher level thinking skills (sequencing, comparing/contrasting, analyzing)
3- Perceptive: uses a limited number of strategies and sources to investigate; sees possible perspectives; makes basic connections outside of context
2- Literal: directed research; retelling; minimal sequencing of information; simplistic analyzing; limited connections within context
1- Naive: no strategies for conducting research; unimaginative; unable to draw conclusions; does not go beyond minimal expectations; makes no connections

---

4. Self-Directed Learning: Journaling, Research, Creation, Presenting, Reflection, etc.

4- Independent: self-motivated; takes initiative; resilient; leads and teaches others; meaningful reflections with new insights; team player; peer role model
3- Involved: works around obstacles; good insights; flexible; works with others
2- Interested: reluctant; limited insights; inflexible; easily flustered or frustrated; easily distracted
1- Dependent: easily discouraged; low motivation; lack of confidence; little or no insight; unaware of what he or she does not know; unfocused

(Continued)

(Continued)

5. Responsible Citizenship: Peer Reflection, Community Service, Presentation to Others, etc.

4- Effective Collaboration: ethical; honest; sets goals and establishes deadlines; persistent; understands the value of responsibility and citizenship; empathetic; encourages and inspires others

3- Sufficient Collaboration: ethical; honest; meets deadlines; is understanding and aware of others; contributes productively and responsibly

2- Inconsistent Collaboration: motivated only when personally interested; low work ethic; misses deadlines; errors; aware of others, but self-centered

1- Inadequate Collaboration: no self-motivation; follows others; lacks ethical standards; disrupts the learning process of others; no work ethic; does not meet deadlines; plagiarizes; insensitive; unaware of community needs

Example produced by Valor Middle School Encore Teaching Team

RESOURCE O

Culminating Demonstration Rubric for First-Grade Students at Heritage Elementary

	Excelling	Meeting Standards	Developing	Emerging
Ideas, content, and meaning	• My purpose and main idea are very clear, and I use carefully selected, accurate, and varied details. • I use meaningful, vivid, and juicy content vocabulary that energizes my writing. • I write a variety of interesting sentences that flow together naturally.	• My purpose and main idea are clear, and I include varied details. • I use meaningful and juicy content vocabulary. • I write a variety of sentences that make sense and fit together.	• My purpose and main idea are not very clear. I use limited, unfocused details. • I try to use juicy words. • I sometimes write in simple sentences that do not make sense to me or to others when I read them out loud.	• My purpose and main idea are unclear, and I only list a few details. • I use repetitive words that make my writing boring. • I only write simple, repetitive sentences that do not go together.
Organization and conventions	• I organize my ideas thoughtfully to achieve my purpose. • I effectively edit my writing. • My writing has a creative introduction, informative and descriptive middle, and a satisfying ending. • I use correct spelling, punctuation, and capitalization. • My printed work is attractive and neatly presented.	• I make an effective plan for my writing. • I edit my writing. • My writing has a clear beginning and ending. The middle is complete. • I use correct spelling, punctuation, and capitalization. • My printed work is neat with correctly formed letters.	• I make a simple plan for my writing. • I edit my writing but make few changes. • My writing is missing the beginning or ending. The middle may be incomplete. • I spell simple words but use inventive spelling to write more complex words. I sometimes use correct punctuation and capitalization. • My printed work is readable but messy.	• I try to make a plan. • I edit without purpose. • My writing is missing a beginning and an ending. The middle is weak. • Others cannot read my writing because of spelling, punctuation, and capitalization errors. • My printed work lacks neatness and is difficult to read.

(Continued)

(Continued)

	Excelling	Meeting Standards	Developing	Emerging
Oral language	• I speak enthusiastically about my topic, organize my ideas effectively, and have a strong closing to engage my listeners. • I speak easily and confidently in front of my listeners because I am prepared and practiced. • I capture my listeners' attention with an interesting opening that inludes the title or subject.	• I speak clearly and smoothly and I organize my ideas to hold the listeners' attention. • I speak easily in front of my listeners because I am prepared and practiced. • I open my presentation with the title or subject.	• I speak too softly, giggle, rarely stay on topic, and have a hard time holding listeners' attention. • I practiced, but it is difficult for me. • I just talk about my subject.	• I have a hard time speaking in front of others. • I am not ready. • It is difficult for me to talk about my subject.

RESOURCE P

Kindergarten Literacy Lesson Plans

Things to Consider When Planning
1. Standards, benchmarks, competencies, and concepts from map and unit design 2. Engager—How will we get students' attention? Bridge from previous day? Build background? 3. What do we want students to learn today? 4. Which informal assessments are we going to use? When? 5. Which cognitive strategies are we using in this lesson? 6. How will we build vocabulary and oral language proficiency? 7. What reading and writing strategies will we use? Are they connected? 8. Which instructional strategies are essential? 9. Which centers will we use for student practice? How will students practice? 10. What materials do wc need? 11. How will we ask students to review and reflect?

Unit: *Winter/"un dia de Nieve"*		Objectives—Language-ELD-What children will learn: *retelling, vocabulary, sequencing*	
Cognitive strategies: *schema*		Building background: *schema/KWL chart (add to it)*	
Informal assessments: *observation, participation, taking notes*		Building vocabulary/key vocabulary: *brainstorming ideas, labeling vocabulary/classification*	
Student practice: *Big group and center*			
Reading strategies: *read-aloud, model, shared, guided, independent, reading workshop* Mini-lesson: *sequencing, concept of print, phonemic awareness, visual—sensory images*		Writing strategies: *model, shared, interactive, guided, independent, writer's workshop, writing traits, four-square* Mini-lesson: *model four-square writing with guided writing, four-square independent writing*	
Instructional strategies, adaptations KWL *Hands on activity* *Visualization*		Materials: *Book "Un Dia de Nieve"* *Visuals: flash cards* *White boards* *Center materials*	
How will students review and reflect? *Oral development and four-square writing*			
Centers 1. *Listening center—"Un dia de Nieve" Draw three things that happen in the story* | 1 | 2 | 3 |	2. *Storybook writing center—Snow Man* 8 Hombres	3. *Art center Tri-dimensional model of story, "Un dia de Nieve"*	4. *Snow puzzles*

(Continued)

(Continued)

5. "Ropa de Invierno" Vocabulary	6. Reading center—Various winter seasono story books		

No School	Tuesday	Wednesday	Thursday	Friday
	—Brainstorm using students schema, —Use visual (poster) too help with the idea.	—Introduce the book and add to the list—what Peter was doing in the story. (Activities) —Compare/contrast some different vocabulary and phrases.	—Review the story. —Apply strategies mentioned previously. —Introduce four square writing in big group. ⊢⊟Winter⊟⊣ Que me gusta hacer en el invierno?	—Review four Square writing. —Independent four Square on their white boards. —Activity in circle with big group. —Use chart to review ideas. —Have students share with the class in a large circle.

References

Ackerman, R. H., & Mackenzie, S. V. (Eds.). (2007). *Uncovering teacher leadership: Essays and voices from the field.* Thousand Oaks, CA: Corwin Press.

Ainsworth, L. (2003a). *Power standards: Identifying the standards that matter the most.* Englewood, CO: Advanced Learning Press.

Ainsworth, L. (2003b). *Unwrapping the standards: A simple process to make standards manageable.* Englewood, CO: Advanced Learning Press.

Anderson, R. C., & Pearson, P. D. (1984). A schema—Theoretic view of basic processes in reading. In P. D. Pearson, R. Barr, M. L. Kamil, & P. Mosenthal (Eds.), *Handbook of reading research* (pp. 255–291). White Plains, NY: Longman.

Annenberg Institute for School Reform. (Producer). (1997). *Looking at student work: A window into the classroom.* [Motion picture]. (Available from the Annenberg Institute for School Reform, Brown University, Box 1985, Providence, RI 02912)

Benjamin, A. (2002). *Differentiated instruction: A guide for middle and high school teachers.* Larchmont, NY: Eye on Education.

Biggs, J. B. (1999). *Teaching for quality learning at university: What the student does.* Buckingham, UK: Society for Research in Higher Education.

Blankstein, A. M. (2004). *Failure is not an option: Six principles that guide student achievement in high-performing schools.* Thousand Oaks, CA: Corwin Press.

Bloom, B. S. (1976). *Human characteristics and school learning.* New York: McGraw-Hill.

Brookhart, S. M. (2004). *Grading.* Upper Saddle River, NJ: Merrill/Prentice Hall.

Brown, W., Rust. C., & Gibbs, G. (1994). Involving students in the assessment process. In *Strategies for diversifying assessment in higher education* (section 5). Oxford Centre for Staff Development. Retrieved September 28, 2008, from http://www.londonmet.ac.uk/deliberations/ocsld-publications/div-ass5.cfm

Bruner, J. (1986). *Actual minds, possible worlds.* Cambridge, MA: Harvard University Press.

Buck Institute for Learning. (n.d.). *Project based learning.* Retrieved September 19, 2008, from http://www.bie.org/index.php/site/PBL/overview_pbl/

Caine, R. N., & Caine, G. (1994). *Making connections.* Menlo Park, CA: Addison Wesley.

Caine, R. N., Caine, G., McClintic, C., & Klimek, K. (2005). *12 Brain/mind learning principles in action.* Thousand Oaks, CA: Corwin Press.

Calkins, L. M. (1991). *Living between the lines.* Portsmouth, NH: Heinemann.

Carlson, M. O., Humphrey, G. E., & Reinhardt, K. S. (2003). *Weaving science inquiry and continuous assessment.* Thousand Oaks, CA: Corwin Press.

Center for Collaborative Education. (2001, January). Looking collaboratively at student and teacher work. *Turning points: Transforming middle schools.* Boston: National Turning Points Center. Retrieved September 07, 2008, from http://www.turningpts.org/pdf/LASW.pdf

Chappuis S., & Chappuis J. (2007, December/2008, January). The best value in formative assessment. *Educational leadership, 65*(4), 14–18.

Chappuis, S., Stiggins, R. J., Arter, J., & Chappuis, J. (2005). *Assessment for learning: An action guide for school leaders.* Portland, OR: Assessment Training Institute.

Churchill, W. (Speaker). (1940). Speech delivered to Parliament. *BBC On this day*. Retrieved September 27, 2008, from http://news.bbc.co.uk/onthisday/low/dates/stories/june/4/newsid_3500000/3500865.stm

Costa, A. L. (2008). *The school as a home for the mind: Creating mindful curriculum, instruction, and dialogue* (2nd ed.). Thousand Oaks, CA: Corwin Press.

Costa, A. L., & Kallick, B. (2000). *Assessing and reporting on habits of the mind*. Alexandria, VA: Association for Supervision and Curriculum Development.

Covey, S. R. (2005). *The 8th habit*. New York: Free Press.

Dalton, J., & Boyd, J. (1992). *I teach: A guide to inspiring classroom leadership*. Portsmouth, NH: Heinemann.

Daniels, H., Bizar, M., & Zemelman, S. (2001). *Rethinking the high school: Best practice in teaching, learning, and leadership*. Portsmouth, NH: Heinemann.

Daniels, H., & Zemelman, S. (2004). *Subject matters: Every teachers' guide to content-area reading*. Portsmouth, NY: Heinemann.

Dewey, J. (1966). *Democracy and education: An introduction to the philosophy of education*. New York: Free Press.

DuFour, R., & Eaker, R. (1998). *Professional learning communities at work*. Alexandria, VA: Association for Supervisors and Curriculum Development.

DuFour, R., Eaker, R., Karhanek, G., & DuFour, R. (2004). *Whatever it takes: How professional learning communities respond when kids don't learn*. Bloomington, IN: National Education Service.

Earl, L. (2003). *Assessment strategies for self-directed learning*. Thousand Oaks, CA: Corwin.

Easton, L. B. (2008). *Powerful designs for professional learning* (2nd ed.). Oxford, OH: National Staff Development Council.

Eastwood, C., Haggis, P., Lorenz, R., & Spielberg, S. (Producers), Eastwood, C. (Director), & Yamashita, I. (Writer). (2006). *Letters from Iwo Jima* [Motion Picture]. United States: Amblin Entertainment.

Edelman, M. W. (1992). *The measure of our success: A letter to my children and yours*. Boston: Beacon Press.

Edmonds, R. (1979). Effective schools for the urban poor. *Educational Leadership, 37*(10), 15–24.

Elbow, P. (1980). *Writing without teachers*. Oxford, OH: Oxford Press.

English, F., & Steffy, B. E. (2001). *Deep curriculum alignment*. Lanham, MD: Scarecrow Press.

Erickson, H. L. (2002). *Concept-based curriculum and instruction: Teaching beyond the facts*. Thousand Oaks, CA: Corwin Press.

Frank, A. (1952). *The diary of a young girl* (B. M. Mooyaart-Doubleday, Trans.). London: Constellation Books.

Freiberg, K., & Frieberg, J. (1996). *NUTS! Southwest Airlines' crazy recipe for business and personal success*. Austin, TX: Bard Press.

Friedman, T. L. (2005). *The world is flat*. New York: Farrar, Straus and Giroux.

Gallagher, C. W., & Ratzlaff, S. (2007, December/2008, January). The road less traveled. *Education Leadership, 65*(4), 48–53.

Gallagher, K. (2004). *Deeper reading: Comprehending challenging texts, grades 4–12*. Portland, MA: Stenhouse.

Gittell, J. H. (2003). *The Southwest Airline way: Using the power of relationships to achieve high performance*. New York: McGraw Hill.

Giuliani, R. W. (2002). *Leadership*. New York: Hyperion.

Glatthorn, A. (2000). *The principal as curriculum leader*. Thousand Oaks, CA: Corwin Press.

Graves, D. (1983). *Writing: Teachers and children at work*. Portsmouth, NH: Heinemann.

Graves, D. (2002). *Testing is not teaching*. Portsmouth, NH: Heinemann.

Guskey, T. R. (1997). *Implementing mastery learning*. New York: Wadsworth.

Guskey, T. R. (2000). Grading policies that work against standards . . . and how to fix them. *NASSP Bulletin, 84*(620), 20–29.

Guskey, T. R. (2007, December/2008, January). The rest of the story. *Education Leadership, 65*(4), 28–35.

Guskey, T. R., & Bailey, J. M. (2001). *Developing grading and reporting systems for student learning.* Thousand Oaks, CA: Corwin Press.

Haladyna, T. M. (1999). *A complete guide to student grading.* Boston: Allyn and Bacon.

Hall, G., & Hord, S. (2001). *Implementing change: Patterns, principles, and potholes.* Boston: Allyn and Bacon.

Harwayne, S. (1999). *Going public: Priorities & practices at the Manhattan New School.* Portsmouth, NY: Heinemann.

Hirsh, S., & Killion, J. (2007). *The leading educator.* Oxford, OH: National Staff Development Council.

Hord, S., & Sommers, W. A. (2008). *Leading professional learning communities: Voices from research and practice.* Thousand Oaks, CA: Corwin Press in joint publication with National Association of Secondary School Principals and National Staff Development Council.

Jensen, E. (1998). *Teaching with the brain in mind.* Alexandria, VA: Association for Supervision and Curriculum Development.

Keene, E. O., & Zimmermann, S. (1997). *Mosaic of thought.* Portsmouth, NH: Heinemann.

Killion, J., & Harrison, J. (2006). *Taking the lead: New roles for teachers and school-based coaches.* Oxford, OH: National Staff Development Council.

Koretz, D. (2002, October). No child left behind? *Harvard Graduate School of Education News.* Retrieved September 08, 2008, from http://www.gse.harvard.edu/news/features/koretz10012002.html

Lambert, L. (1998). *Building leadership capacity in schools.* Alexandria, VA: Association for Supervision and Curriculum Development.

Loehr, J. & Schwartz, T. (2003). *The power of full engagement.* New York: The Free Press.

Many, T., & King, D. (2008, Summer). Districts speak with one voice: Clarity and coherence comes from professional learning communities, *JSD, 29*(3) 28–32.

Marzano, R. (2000). *Transforming classroom grading.* Alexandria, VA: Association for Supervisors and Curriculum Development.

Marzano, R. J. (2007). *The art and science of teaching.* Alexandria, VA: Association for Supervision and Curriculum Development.

Marzano, R., Waters, T., & Mcnulty, B. A. (2005). *School leadership that works: From research to results.* Alexandria, VA: Association for Supervisors and Curriculum Development.

Miller, D. (2002). *Reading with meaning: Teaching comprehension in the primary grades.* Portsmouth, NH: Heinemann.

National Center for Educational Statistics. (2004, August). *English Language Learner Students in U.S. Public Schools, 1994–2000.* Jessup, MD: U.S. Department of Education.

National Commission on Writing in America's Schools and Colleges. (2003, April). *The neglected "R."* Retrieved September 28, 2008, from http://www.writingcommission.org/prod_downloads/writingcom/neglectedr.pdf

National Council of Teachers of English. (November, 2004). *NCTE Beliefs about the teaching of writing.* Available at www.ncte.org

National Education Business Coalition, The Partnership for 21st Century Skills. (n.d.). Retrieved September 28, 2008, from www.21stcenturyskills.org

National Research Council. (1999). *How people learn: Bridging research and practice.* M. S. Donovan, J. D. Bransford, & J. W. Pellegrino (Eds.). Washington, DC: National Academy Press.

National Research Council. (2005). *How students learn mathematics in the classroom.* Washington, DC: National Academy Press.

Palincsar, A. S., & Brown, A. L. (1984). Reciprocal teaching of comprehension—Fostering and monitoring activity. *Cognition and Instruction, 1,* 117–175.

Palmer, P. J. (2007). *The courage to teach: Exploring the inner landscape of a teacher's life.* San Francisco: John Wiley & Sons.

Patterson, K., Grenny, J., McMillan, R., & Switzler, A. (2002). *Crucial conversations: Tools for talking when stakes are high.* New York: McGraw-Hill.

Perkins, D. N. T., Holtman, M. P., Kessler, P. R., & McCarthy, C. (2000). *Leading at the edge: Leadership lessons from the extraordinary saga of Shackleton's Antarctic expedition.* NY: Amacom.

Piaget, J. (1974). *Origins of intelligence in children*. Madison, CT: International University Press.

Piercy, T. D. (2006). *Compelling conversations: Connecting leadership to student achievement*. Englewood, CO: Advanced Learning Press.

Project Lead the Way. Retrieved September 28, 2008, from www.projectleadtheway.org

Psencik, K., Czaplicki, H. J., Houston, T. A., & Kopp, D. (2007, Fall). Best practices: Campaign to discover practices nets gains for high school. *JSD, 28*(4), 14–18.

Raphael, T. E. (1984). Teaching learners about sources of information for answering comprehension questions. *Journal of Reading, 27*, 303–311.

Resnick, L. (1984). *Education and learning to think*. London: Falmer Press.

Resnick, L. B., & Resnick, D. P. (1992). Assessing and the thinking curriculum: New tools for educational reform. In B. R. Gifford & M. C. Conner (Eds.), *Changing assessments: Alternative views of aptitude, achievement and instruction* (pp. 37–76). Boston: Kluwer Academic Press.

Richardson, J. (2001, February). *Student work at the core of teacher learning. Results*. Retrieved September 28, 2008, from http://www.nsdc.org/library/publications/results/res2–01rich.cfm

Ritchhart, R. (2002). *Intellectual character: What it is, why it matters, and how to get it*. San Francisco: Jossey-Bass.

Routman, R. (2000). *Conversations*. Portsmouth, NH: Heinemann.

Roy, P., & Hord, S. (Project Directors). (2003). *Moving NSDC standards into practice: Innovation configurations*. Oxford, OH: National Staff Development Council.

Ruzzo, K., & Sacco, M. A. (2004). *Significant studies for second grade: Reading and writing investigations for children*. Portsmouth, NH: Heinemann.

Schlechty, P. C. (1997). *Inventing better schools: An action plan for educational reform*. San Francisco: Jossey-Bass.

Schmoker, M. (2006). *Results now*. Alexandria, VA: Association for Supervision and Curriculum Development.

Scott, S. (2002). *Fierce conversations: Achieving success at work & in life, one conversation at a time*. New York: Berkley Books.

Senge, P. (2000). *Schools that learn*. New York: Doubleday.

Sergiovanni, T. J. (1992). *Moral leadership: Getting to the heart of school improvement*. San Francisco: Jossey-Bass.

Silver, H. F., Strong, R. W., & Perini, M. J. (2000). *So each may learn: Integrated learning styles and multiple intelligences*. Alexandria, VA: Association for Supervision and Curriculum Development.

Smilkstein, R. (2003). *We're born to learn*. Thousand Oaks, CA: Corwin Press.

Sparks, D. (2006). *Leading for results* (2nd ed.). Thousand Oaks, CA: Corwin Press and Oxford, OH: National Staff Development Council.

Sparks, D. (2007, January 8). Professional learning's "APGAR." *Leading and learning: Dennis Sparks, NSDC emeritus executive director writes about leadership and professional learning in K–12 schools and systems*. Retrieved October 8, 2008, from http://www.nsdc.org/sparksblog/2007/01/professional-learnings-apgar_08.html

Sparks, D., & Hirsh, S. (1997). *A new vision for staff development*. Oxford, OH: National Staff Development Council.

Sprenger, M. (1999). *Learning and memory*. Alexandria, VA: Association for Supervision and Curriculum Development.

Sternberg, R. (2007, December/2008, January). Assessing what matters most. *Educational leadership, 65*(4), 20–26.

Stiggins, R. (1997). *Student-centered classroom assessment*. Upper Saddle River, NJ: Prentice-Hall.

Stiggins, R., Arter, J., Chappuis, J., & Chappuis, S. (2007). *Classroom assessment for student learning: Doing it right—Using it well*. Upper Saddle River, NJ: Assessment Training Institute.

Stigler, J. W., & Hiebert, J. (1999). *The teaching gap*. New York: Free Press.

Sylwester, R. (1995). *A celebration of neurons*. Alexandria, VA: Association for Supervision and Curriculum Development.

Tate, M. (2003). *Worksheets don't grow dendrites: Instructional strategies that engage the brain.* Thousand Oaks, CA: Corwin Press.

Tichy, N. M. (2002). *The cycle of leadership.* New York: HarperCollins.

Tomlinson, C. (2007, December/2008, January). Learning to love assessment. *Educational Leadership, 65*(4), 20–26.

Von Glasersfeld, E. (1989). Cognition, construction of knowledge, and teaching. *Synthese, 80,* 121–140.

Vygotsky, L. S. (1978). *Mind in society: The development of higher psychological processes.* Cambridge, MA: Harvard University Press.

WebQuest. (n.d.). Retrieved September 19, 2008, from www.WebQuest.org

Wertsch, J. V. (1985). *Vygotsky and the formation of the mind.* Cambridge, MA: Harvard University Press.

Wheatley, M. (1992). *Leadership and the new science.* San Francisco: Berrett-Koehler.

Wheatley, M. (2002). *Turning to one another.* San Francisco: Berrett-Koehler.

Wiggins, G. (1993). *Assessing student performance: Exploring the purpose and limits of testing.* San Francisco: Jossey-Bass.

Wiggins, G., & McTighe, J. (1998). *Understanding by design.* Alexandria, VA: Association for Supervision and Curriculum Development.

Wilson, J., & Jan, L. (1993). *Thinking for themselves: Developing strategies for reflective learning.* Prahran, Australia: Eleanor Curtain.

Yunus, M. (2007). *Creating a world without poverty: Social business and the future of capitalism.* New York: Public Affairs.

Index

CORWIN

A SAGE Company

The Corwin logo—a raven striding across an open book—represents the union of courage and learning. Corwin is committed to improving education for all learners by publishing books and other professional development resources for those serving the field of PreK–12 education. By providing practical, hands-on materials, Corwin continues to carry out the promise of its motto: **"Helping Educators Do Their Work Better."**